Iceland

Text: Lance Price and James Proctor
Editors: Jane Hutchings and Clare Peel
Principal photographer: Lance Price
Cover photograph: Powerstock
Layout Concept: Klaus Geisler
Picture Editor: Hilary Genin
Managing Editor: Clare Peel
Series Editor: Tony Halliday

Berlitz® POCKET GUIDE

Iceland

First Edition 2004

Photography by:
Apa/Lance Price 9, 10, 14, 16, 19, 20, 25, 29, 30, 41, 42, 44, 55, 56, 57, 60, 61, 64, 65, 66, 69, 72, 74, 77, 79, 80, 81, 83, 93, 98, 100, 103; Icelandic Tourist Board 39; Icelandic Tourist Board/Photo: www.bluelagoon.is 6, 37; Icelandic Tourist Board/Photo: BKN Studios 12; Icelandic Tourist Board/Photo: Dieter Schweizer 22, 47, 48, 51, 52/3, 54, 76, 82, 88; Icelandic Tourist Board/Photo: Randall Hyman 26, 27, 33, 34, 49, 78, 86, 90, 96, 99, 105; Icelandic Tourist Board/Photo: Thierry des Ouches 50; Icelandic Tourist Board/Photo: Ruth Gundahl Madsen 59, 70; Icelandic Tourist Board/Photo: Frederic Reglain 87; Icelandic Tourist Board/Photo: www.adventure.is 95; Hans Klüche 31, 43, 45, 75, 67, 94; Cathleen Naundorf 62, 100

CONTACTING THE EDITORS
Every effort has been made to provide accurate information in this publication, but changes are inevitable. The publisher cannot be responsible for any resulting loss, inconvenience or injury. We would appreciate it if readers would call our attention to any errors or outdated information by contacting Berlitz Publishing, PO Box 7910, London SE1 1WE, England. Fax: (44) 20 7403 0290; e-mail: berlitz@apaguide.co.uk www.berlitzpublishing.com

Iceland's geysers (page 42) are unfailing crowd-pleasers

The geothermal wonders of the interior (page 85) include bubbling hot pools

Surrounded by volcanic peaks, Lake Mývatn (page 66) is a walkers' paradise

Iceland is a popular destination for bird-watchers. The country's largest puffin colony is on the island of Heimaey (page 45)

TOP TEN ATTRACTIONS

The naturally heated waters of the Blue Lagoon are renowned for their therapeutic effects (page 37)

The extraordinary iceberg-studded glacial lagoon, Jökulsárlón (page 52) is simply out of this world

Colonies of Arctic tern inhabit Reynisdrangar, the peculiar black 'Troll Rocks' at Vík (page 49)

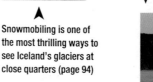

Snowmobiling is one of the most thrilling ways to see Iceland's glaciers at close quarters (page 94)

The 20th-century Hallgrímskirkja, with its sweeping spire, is a major landmark of the capital, Reykjavík (page 25)

Iceland's many spectacular waterfalls include Goðafoss (page 65)

CONTENTS

A ➤ in the text denotes a highly recommended sight

Fact Sheets

INTRODUCTION

Few places on earth can match the raw and intense beauty of Iceland. Both fiery and cold, forbidding and inviting, it is a place of dramatic contrasts, home to immense ice fields, bubbling mud pools, colossal waterfalls and hot springs. Although Iceland has a long, rich cultural history, it is the land itself, sculpted by the forces of nature into a unique, ever-changing landscape, that tells the country's true story.

Underground Drama

In geological terms, Iceland is a mere babe, composed of some of the youngest rocks on earth and still being formed. Over the centuries, eruptions have spewed vast fields of lava across the island's surface and projected choking clouds of ash high into the air, blocking out the sunlight and blighting crops. Recent eruptions have been less destructive, but no less spectacular, than earlier ones; every day there are thousands of minor earthquakes and small shocks, most of which are only detectable by seismologists.

The presence of so much natural energy just below ground makes it possible not just to see the awesome power of nature, but to feel, hear and smell it. The limitless reserves of geothermal energy that have produced such a varied terrain also supply heat and power to Iceland's homes, and the 'rotten egg' smell of sulphur is unmistakable. Dams across

Iceland straddles the North Atlantic Ridge where two of the tectonic plates making up the Earth's surface are slowly drifting apart. The country is widening at a rate of roughly 1cm (⅓ in) annually. Along this fault line, from the northeast to the southwest, earthquakes and volcanic activity are commonplace.

fast-flowing glacial rivers provide the nation with more than enough hydroelectrically generated power to meet its needs.

The abundant hot water not only heats homes and offices, in winter it is piped under pavements in the centre of Reykjavík to melt away the snow and ice. And year round it contributes to the social life of the Icelanders, filling outdoor swimming pools, where people meet to take a little exercise or just to chat in the hot tubs and steam rooms.

Pollution-Free Land

For Icelanders, keeping their landscape clean and pollution-free is a top priority. It's with justifiable pride that they boast that the water from any stream or non-glacial river in the country is drinkable, due in no small part to the lack of heavy industry. Even in the capital, Reykjavík, the air is bitingly clean. You won't see rubbish tipped at the wayside here, nor will you encounter widespread burning of fossil fuels. Recently, the government has attempted to attract new heavy industry such as aluminum smelting, which needs high amounts of energy; however, the environmental impact of the new dams that would be required have roused huge controversy.

The Icelandic Horse

Horses have been used for transport and farming in Iceland for over 1,000 years. The country's isolation and a ban on importing new horses to keep out disease means that its horse population is remarkably pure. Icelandic horses are relatively small but extremely tough and they can handle the rugged terrain with ease. They are found in a wide variety of colours and are respected worldwide for their intelligence, stamina and speed. The Icelandic horse has a unique gait, known as a *tölt* – a kind of running walk with a gentle flowing movement that makes for a very smooth and comfortable ride.

Icelandic horses thrive in rugged terrain

High Standard of Living

Iceland is a European nation, although it remains outside the European Union mainly to protect its economically vital fishing grounds. It has strong social institutions and a well-funded welfare system. Few Icelanders are conspicuously rich, but there's little urban poverty, and the standard of living throughout the country is high.

Geographically equal in size to England, Iceland has only approximately 283,000 inhabitants, half of whom live in and around the capital. Icelanders have a powerful respect for nature and know they can never expect to control it or have it all to themselves. The shy Arctic fox and the reindeer are rarely seen, but sheep are plentiful, and horses are widely kept. Millions of seabirds flock to the country's cliff tops and coastal meadows to nest during the bright summer months, while offshore, whales, dolphins and seals are abundant in some of the cleanest waters on earth.

Precious catch

Icelanders make the most of the many benefits of their extraordinary environment, spending as much time as possible outdoors, weather-permitting. Walking, climbing and horseriding are popular pursuits, and, as the importance of tourism has grown, so too has the number of companies offering snowmobiling on the glaciers, hiking adventures in the interior and whale-watching off the coast.

Reykjavík

Dominated by brightly painted buildings and a massive central church, Reykjavík is a lively place. Here a modern, cosmopolitan city has evolved beneath the snow-capped mountains. The population may be small, but it's clear from the cafés, restaurants and nightclubs that this is a place where people know how to have a good time. However, the scene starts late, and the often eye-watering prices for alcohol and a decent meal force many locals to get their eating and a fair bit of their drinking done at home before they venture out.

Outside the capital, some towns, notably Akureyri in the north, share some of Reykjavík's energy, but most are happy not even to try. The smaller towns are quiet, compact and neat, often no more than a cluster of colourful houses around a church or shop. The pace of life is slow, and the sense of community strong.

Hot Springs and Outdoor Baths

Since the late 1970s the country's only major road, a vast circular route around the coast, has linked village to town, countryside to capital. Most communities are found on or near the ring road, a short distance from the sea, where the land is at its flattest and most fertile. This narrow coastal plain, the only truly habitable part of the country, makes up just one-fifth of Iceland's total area.

Fortunately, much of the most impressive scenery is easily accessible from the ring road. The site of the original Geysir, which gave its name to all geysers around the world, is close to the capital, as is the best outdoor bath on the planet, the Blue Lagoon. The mighty Vatnajökull glacier, at 8,400 sq km (3,200 sq miles) the largest in Europe, reaches down to the sea across the southeast of the country.

To the north, Jökulsárgljúfur National Park is not only an impressive tongue-twister, even by Icelandic standards, but also home to Europe's largest, most powerful waterfall, Dettifoss, which plummets into the canyon below amid clouds of rainbow-coloured spray. In the north and west, the coastline is splintered by craggy fjords and the sheer granite

What's in a Name

According to tradition, Iceland owes its name to a Viking adventurer who chanced upon it *circa* AD 870. After spending a long hard winter watching his cattle die from the bitter cold and lack of good grazing, he climbed a mountain only to see the fjord choked with drift ice. Wholly disenchanted, he named the place *Ísland*, literally 'ice land', and promptly departed for the positively balmy climes of his native Norway. Four years later one of his compatriots returned and started the first proper settlement at a place he called Reykjavík, or 'smoky bay', after the plumes of steam he saw rising from nearby thermal springs.

sides of flat tabletop mountains. Further inland, wide valleys rise towards the barren upland plateaux that constitute the interior. This is Europe's last wilderness, a wide expanse of bleak grey lava desert fringed by volcanoes, glaciers and mountaintops, most of it all but inaccessible.

Long Days of Summer

The weather in Iceland can be as varied as the geography. Winters are cold and dark, with a large amount of snowfall. Light relief is provided at night by the spectral glow of the northern lights *(aurora borealis)*. It's only in summer, when the temperatures rise and the long days are often bright and sunny, that it's possible to see the full extent of the country properly. Many of the hotels and restaurants, especially the more affordable ones, are open only between May and September. Similarly, the bus companies don't run a full service until late June, when the last of the snow has gone.

Smoking landscape

Despite the rigours of its landscape, Iceland is a very welcoming place. Its people aren't given to great outward shows of emotion but they are intensely proud of their country and will offer an embrace that is as sincere as it is warm to the visitor who's willing to respect their land.

A BRIEF HISTORY

While elsewhere in Europe, civilizations, empires and dynasties came and went, Iceland remained uninhabited and undiscovered. It wasn't until the 8th century AD that Irish monks became the first people known to have set foot on the island, relishing its solitude. They left no physical trace behind either, nor, being all men, any new generation. Within 100 years the peace they had enjoyed was no longer: the Vikings were coming. Much of Iceland's history was chronicled within a few hundred years of the events happening. The *Landnámabók* (Book of Settlements), written in the 12th century, describes in detail the first permanent inhabitants. The sagas, dramatic tales of early Iceland penned 100 years later, give a lot more colour to the story in the form of fiction.

The First Settlers

The country's first settlers were Norwegians escaping political persecution and economic hardship at home. They found Iceland by accident, having already colonised parts of both Scotland and the Faroe Islands. The official 'First Settler' was Ingólfur Arnarson, who enjoyed his first winter so much that in 874 he went to fetch his extended family and friends to come and join him. They brought with them farm animals, paganism and Irish slaves, some of whom would cause mutiny and kill their owners.

Although many Icelanders can trace their families back to the early settlers, family names do not exist. Instead, children absorb their father's first name into their own. A man named Eiríkur Gúðbrandsson might, for example, have a son named Leifur Eiríksson and a daughter named Þórdís Eiríksdóttir.

Viking armour

However, there was no indigenous population for the colonisers to evict or butcher, and the biggest threat they faced was from the elements.

These first Icelanders established farms in the rather more hospitable parts of the country, and within 60 years there were approximately 25,000 people living around the coast. Some basic laws were already in place: a man could claim as much land as he could light bonfires around in one day, so long as each one could be seen from the others. Women could have as much land as a heifer could walk around in a day. Inevitably disputes broke out, which the local chieftains had to resolve. When they failed, there could be bloody battles.

The First Parliament

In AD 930 the chieftains got together and agreed on a relatively democratic system of government. A Commonwealth was established, with a national assembly or *Alþingi* meeting for two weeks every summer at Þingvellir. Here, new laws would be agreed and infringements of old laws settled by a system of regional courts. The worst punishment was to be declared an outlaw and banished from the country.

The system wasn't perfect, and there were still some bloody battles – these were, after all, the descendants of

Vikings, who valued courage and honour above all else. Nonetheless this period is now considered to have been a Golden Age, the Saga Age, full of great heroes and wise men.

From Pagans to Christians

Soon, however, things were to change dramatically. Christianity had spread to northern Europe, and the zealous, if bloodthirsty, King Ólafur Tryggvason of Norway wanted Iceland for the new religion too. When his missionaries encountered resistance in the late 10th century he was all for butchering the entire population until the Icelandic chieftain Gizur the White promised to have another go by more peaceful means. Fortunately the lawspeaker, who presided over the Alþingi, was at that time the widely respected Þorgeir. He persuaded both sides to agree to accept his decision in advance and then went off to meditate. He came back and announced that Iceland would become Christian, although pagans could continue to practise their beliefs in private.

Bishoprics, monasteries and schools quickly followed, and books were soon being written for the first time. As a sign of their independence the writers chose to do their work in Icelandic, not Latin. There were so few foreign influences in the centuries to come that the language they used is almost identical to the Icelandic spoken today.

All was not well in the land, however, and Iceland was about to enter its Dark Age. The Hekla volcano outside Reykjavík erupted in 1104, burying nearby farms; over-grazing and soil erosion from excessive tree-felling further reduced the amount of viable land. At the same time the church became greedy and, by imposing tithes, it split the formerly egalitarian society. Some chiefs, who were given church lands or made into senior clergy, found themselves increasingly rich and powerful. Before long the most important families started fighting for supremacy. The Alþingi, which had relied on people voluntarily

Illustration from *Njals Saga*

accepting its authority, was now powerless to respond.

Civil War and Black Death

Soon the country was in a state of civil war, which was ended only when Norway took sovereignty to help maintain order in 1262. Iceland kept many of its old laws, but 700 years of foreign domination had begun.

Revolts and skirmishes continued, while nature also took its toll. Harsh winters destroyed farm animals and crops, yet more eruptions covered parts of the country in ash, and the Black Death arrived in Iceland, laying waste to half the population.

Those Icelanders still living were too busy struggling to survive to notice that Denmark had taken over the Norwegian throne and was therefore their new master. But the Danes took little interest in their new acquisition, despite it possessing something the rest of Europe suddenly wanted: cod. Fishing brought new wealth to coastal landowners, but it brought new trouble, too.

English and German adventurers started appearing offshore, fighting among themselves, indulging in piracy and trying to control the trade in dried cod. The English got the upper hand, and this became known as the English Century. The Danes eventually realised that they were losing out financially. When Denmark tried to ban the English from the country, the latter killed the governor and started bringing in their canons. By 1532, however, the tide had turned, and the English leader was killed in renewed fighting with Germany. From then on England let the Danes and Germans fight among themselves and turned their attentions elsewhere.

The Reformation

The Church was still a dominant force in the early 16th century, and when Scandinavia turned Lutheran in the 1530s it was inevitable that Iceland would soon follow suit. By the middle of the century the Protestant Reformation had been well and truly imposed on an unwilling population.

By this time, Denmark was gaining increased political authority over Iceland, and eventually complete control of the country was passed to Copenhagen. From 1602 all of Iceland's

The Sagas

Between the 12th and 15th centuries some of the great stories the Icelanders had previously passed on from generation to generation were written down. Collectively known as *The Sagas* (literally 'things told'), they are some of the most dramatic and compelling tales in world literature. Scholars argue about how accurate they are, but for good old-fashioned story telling they are unbeatable. Families are torn apart by feuds, knights ride off to battle in shining armour, saints are saintly, the wicked are truly wicked, and mythical dragons and dwarves stalk the land. They are written in an unemotional style that makes the brutal fates of many of their characters even more shocking. The manuscripts were collected for posterity by Árni Magnússon (1663–1730) and taken off to Copenhagen for safety, but most were then lost in a terrible fire. Árni himself braved the flames to rescue some of them. The surviving *Sagas* weren't returned to Iceland until long after Independence. Perhaps wary of their troubled history, the authorities in Reykjavík keep them under lock and key, although some are occasionally put on display at the Culture House.

Jón Sigurðsson (1811–69) is a great hero to Icelanders. A scholar and MP, he agitated for independence from Denmark. He helped to achieve limited home rule, but died long before sovereignty was restored in 1918.

trade had to pass by law through a small group of Danish companies, a move that effectively bankrupted the country. Smallpox then wiped out almost a third of the impoverished population, and, just when it seemed as if matters could not get any worse, thousands more citizens were killed in 1783–4 by massive eruptions that poisoned almost the entire country and caused widespread famine. Denmark considered evacuating the whole surviving population, but decided instead to relax the trading laws a little and give the country a chance to recover.

As it did so, educated Icelanders looked to continental Europe and saw democracy stirring in once-powerful monarchies. Jónas Hallgrímsson, a poet, and Jón Sigurðsson, a historian, started a fledgling independence movement. By 1843 they succeeded in getting the Alþingi, suspended since 1800, revived as a consultative assembly. A decade later trade was freed up completely. Slowly, prosperity started to return.

In 1874 Denmark, now a constitutional monarchy, returned full legislative powers to the Alþingi. The tithe system was abolished, schooling became compulsory, and the fishing industry was allowed to grow and prosper. By 1900 Iceland had its own political parties. In 1904 it was granted Home Rule and in 1918 gained independence in return for keeping the Danish king as monarch.

War and Peace

Iceland, now trading with both England and Germany, stayed neutral in World War I, although its growing economy was hit by the Great Depression of the 1930s. During World War II control of the North Atlantic was a key strategic objective, and first Britain, then the United States, landed forces in Iceland. Denmark was invaded by Germany, and its ties to Iceland were finally cut when full independence was declared on 17 June 1944.

Iceland's strategic location made the new government feel nervous, as the Cold War gripped the western world. In response it joined the UN and then NATO. Still, the decision to allow US forces to return to their wartime bases in 1951 provoked riots in Reykjavík.

When Iceland next went to war, however, it was with a fellow NATO country, Britain. Fortunately nobody was killed, and the so-called Cod Wars, that came and went for 30 years after 1952, were no more than a bit of naval muscle flexing. Britain objected to successive extensions to Iceland's

Jón Sigurðsson, leader of the independence movement

territorial waters and sent patrol boats to protect its trawlers. In 1975 it ordered its frigates to ram Icelandic coastguard ships, which had been cutting the cables of British trawlers. Eventually, in 1985, Iceland got its way, and 325-km (200-mile) limits became the norm worldwide.

Although the European Union's stringent fisheries policy has deterred Iceland from joining that group, since the last quarter of the 20th century the country has been increasingly outward looking, attracting foreign businesses and visitors. In 1986 the world's media descended on Reykjavík for a nuclear summit between presidents Reagan and Gorbachev, which was famously held at the Höfði and raised the country's profile worldwide.

International protests forced Iceland to ban commercial whaling in 1989, although many Icelanders want to resume it. The government is pursuing economic growth, but knows that new heavy industry is unpopular – there has been huge controversy in recent years over plans to build a dam and aluminium plant in the Eastern Highlands.

Thereby lies the dilemma: how to protect the natural beauty of the country and yet allow its economy to keep pace with other European nations. Iceland remains dependent on fishing, but new developments, such as using natural energy to grow hothouse crops, show its willingness to diversify.

An Icelander looks to the future

All in all, Iceland looks to the future as a proud and independent nation, happy to cooperate with the world community, but reluctant to be dictated to by it.

Historical Landmarks

Circa **8th century** AD Irish monks start to settle on 'Thule'.

Circa **870** A Norwegian, Hrafna-Flóki, tries to settle in the West Fjords. Foiled by the harsh winter, he calls the land *Ísland* (Iceland).

874 Ingólfur Arnarson and his family and friends settle on Iceland. They name the settlement Reykjavík (Smoky Bay).

930 Creation of the Alþingi parliament.

1000 Christianity is adopted as Iceland's official religion.

13th and 14th centuries Feuding between Norway and Denmark over the ruling of Iceland. Governing power transferred to Copenhagen.

1389 Huge eruption of Mt Hekla, followed by the Black Death.

15th century 'The English Century': England and Germany battle to control trade in cod and other goods.

1662–1854 Trade monopoly with Denmark.

1783 Eruption of Laki volcano poisons the land and leads to famine.

1800 Danish King abolishes the Alþingi; it is reinstated in 1843.

1874 Denmark gives the Alþingi autonomy over domestic affairs.

1904 Iceland is granted home rule.

1918 Iceland made a sovereign state (with Danish king as its monarch).

1940 The Alþingi announces it has taken over the power of the king of Denmark and will govern Iceland itself.

1944 Independence from Denmark declared on 17 June.

1949 Iceland becomes a founding member of NATO.

1952–76 Cod Wars (1952, 1958, 1972, 1975) with the UK.

1955 Halldór Laxness wins the Nobel Prize for Literature.

1963 Surtsey island created by an underwater volcanic eruption.

1973 Volcanic eruption on Heimaey island.

1986 Reykjavík summit between presidents Reagan and Gorbachev.

1994 Iceland enters the European Economic Area.

2000 Mt Hekla eruption in February; earthquakes in June.

2001 Iceland rejoins the International Whaling Commission.

2002–4 Iceland chairs the Arctic Council to promote sustainable development and conservation in the region.

WHERE TO GO

At first glance Iceland appears to be an easy country to get to grips with. It has a relatively small capital city, and most of the other major sights are dotted around a single main road. However, to truly appreciate the majesty of the land and to explore some of its more remote corners takes time and, in some cases, effort as well. Yet Iceland will always repay the trouble you take to see it properly.

Visitors to this country range from the experienced adventure traveller in search of new challenges to those on a two- or three-day stop-over between Europe and North America. Whether you come for several weeks or just a few days there will be no shortage of things to see and do. Iceland's infrastructure is well designed and works efficiently. So whether you prefer to make your own arrangements or join a commercial excursion you'll find everything you need to make your stay a memorable one.

The tourist industry in Iceland works almost exclusively in English, so a lack of Icelandic is not usually a problem. Facilities are constantly improving, and the number of people now visiting Iceland means there is usually a range of options when it comes to choosing tours or means of transport.

REYKJAVÍK

Most visitors start and end their trip in **Reykjavík**, and many are surprised by how small and insubstantial it can seem. There is virtually no high-rise building, certainly there are no skyscrapers, and the use of corrugated iron and timber in

> Reykjavík is the world's most northerly capital city, at 64.08°N. And at 21.55°W it is Europe's most westerly capital.

Powerful Goðafoss (Fall of the Gods) in northern Iceland

many of the buildings makes them look almost temporary. In fact, the building materials and layout of the city are very practical and, like everything else in Iceland, are designed with the elements in mind.

Half the country's population live in the capital, where they enjoy fresh air and a magnificent location between the bay and the mountains and glaciers of the interior. Apart from a few major roads around the edge of town, the streets are narrow and sometimes steep. Reykjavík is a delight, not just for what it has but for what it doesn't have: traffic jams, pollution, jostling crowds, busy commuters packing the

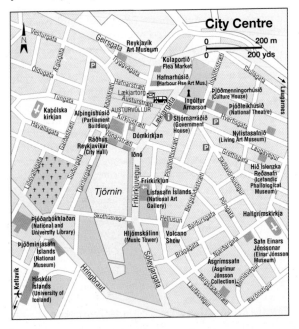

buses and streets. After just a short while you come to realise that Reykjavík manages to have all the best sides of a city – the shops, restaurants, bars and museums – with few of the inconveniences that can make other capitals such hard work. And its manageable size means that almost everything you'll want to see is either within walking distance or a short bus or taxi ride away.

Hallgrímskirkja and Vicinity

The drive into the capital from the airport across the lava fields to the south of the city quickly reveals the central importance of the massive **Hallgrímskirkja** (off Bergþóru-gata; open daily May–Sept 9am–6pm, Oct–Apr 10am–4pm; free). The church is so enormous that it not only dominates the skyline, it reduces everything else to virtual insignificance. The eye is constantly drawn back to it and its bizarre shape resembling a spacecraft ready for lift-off (curiously, once you return to the city the building becomes much less obtrusive). The church is the most obvious place to begin a visit to Reykjavík, and, unless you are staying nearby, you will almost certainly approach it up the steep Skólavörðustígur. As you head up this street, take time to look in the windows of the art galleries that have sprung up here recently, reflecting how much artistic talent such a small country has produced.

Hallgrímskirkja spire

What breath you have left after the climb will be taken away by the sight of Hall-grímskirkja from right up close. Designed by Guðjón

Reykjavík rooftops

Samúelsson, and in almost constant construction since the end of World War II, it is a monument not only to Christ, but also to Reykjavík's belief that being a small city need not limit its ambitions. The steeple is 73m (240ft) high and has a **viewing platform** (open daily 10am–5pm; admission charge) accessed from just inside the door. The church itself is very bare, as befits its Lutheran status, and there is not much to see except the magnificent **organ**, which is 15m (50ft) high and has more than 5,000 pipes.

Just outside the church is a **statue of Leifur Eiríksson**, Iceland's greatest adventurer, who reached America long before Christopher Columbus. The statue was a gift from the US government to mark the Icelandic parliament's 1,000th anniversary in 1930.

The statue is the work of one of Iceland's greatest modern sculptors, Einar Jónsson (1874–1954), and his work can be seen at the nearby **Safn Einars Jónssonar** (Einar Jónsson

Museum, Njarðargata; open June–mid-Sept Tues–Sun 2–5pm, mid-Sept–May Sat, Sun 2–5pm; admission charge). He was virtually a recluse towards the end of his life and many of the 100 or so pieces exhibited here are dark and sombre in character. The entrance is on Freyjugata.

Central Shopping Area

Returning to the bottom of Skólavörðustígur brings you to Reykjavík's main shopping street, **Laugavegur**. This contains a mixture of internationally famous shops, local stores of all kinds and a wide selection of cafés, bars, restaurants and hotels. The street is also home to one of the more unconventional little museums anywhere in the world, the **Hið Islenzka Reðasafn** (Icelandic Phallological Museum, Laugavegur 24; open May–Aug Tues–Sat 2–5pm, Sept–Apr Tues and Sat 2–5pm; admission charge). On display are more than 80 penises from every mammal found in Iceland or in its waters, including whales, horses, foxes and a polar bear that drifted into one of the fjords on an iceberg. Eagerly awaited is the member belonging to a farmer who has promised it to the museum after his death.

A more conventional collection is to be found nearby at the **Þjóðmenningarhúsið** (Culture House, Hverfisgata 15; open daily 11am–5pm; admission charge). This is a fascinating series of exhibits on Icelandic history going right back to the first settlers. You can see the story of the Vikings, some of the manuscripts dating from the 12th and 13th centuries,

Shopping in Laugavegur

including the sagas, and memorabilia from the struggle for independence. It is all housed in a splendid building that was once the National Library.

The Government District

At the western end of the main shopping street, after it changes its name to Bankastræti, is the district devoted to government buildings. These are mostly fairly discreet affairs, since the Icelandic government has seemingly never felt the need to build great monuments to its own importance.

Government House, at the western end of Bankastræti, is not open to the public but is well worth a look from the outside nonetheless. It is one of the oldest houses in the country, dating from 1761 when it was built as a prison. It now houses the office of the prime minister.

On the opposite side of the street there's an imposing **statue of Ingólfur Arnarson**, the first settler, looking out over the Atlantic. Behind him is the National Theatre and to his right are some of the government ministries.

The Icelandic parliament has only 63 members and its headquarters, the **Alþingishúsið** (off Austurvöllur; not open to the public) is almost lost among the surrounding buildings. It is a grey basalt mansion, built in 1881. When parliament is

---

Reykjavik Tourist Card

Before you start exploring the capital, consider investing in a Reykjavík Tourist Card. It can purchased from tourist offices, bus terminals, museums, the City Hall Information Desk and many hotels for a cost of 1000 Ikr for 24 hours, 1500 Ikr for 48 hours and 2000 Isk for 72 hours. The card gives access to 10 museums and galleries, the Family Fun Park and Zoo and all seven of the city's swimming pools. It also entitles the holder to free travel on the city buses.

sitting, its debates are open to the public (Mon–Wed from 1.30pm, Thur from 10.30pm; free) but they are, of course, in Icelandic.

The square behind the parliament, **Austurvöllur**, has pleasant lawns and is a good spot to picnic. You'll be watched over by one of the great campaigners for independence. The **statue of Jón Sigurðsson**, known as *The Pride of Iceland,* rises above the square. A couple of streets away is the main

Dómkirkjan, Reykjavík's cathedral

square, **Lækjartorg**, a lively spot with numerous fast-food outlets and coffee bars.

Alongside the parliament is Reykjavík's Lutheran cathedral **Dómkirkjan** (open Mon–Fri 10am–4pm; free), built in 1785, which has a rather plain façade, but a dramatic interior with arched windows that bathe the place in light.

Just to the west, on the banks of **Tjörnin**, is **Raðhús** (Reykjavík City Hall, corner of Tjarnargata and Vonarstræti; open Mon–Fri 8am–7pm, Sat, Sun noon–6pm; free). Opened in 1992 it's a huge affair in glass and steel and is considered an excellent example of modern Nordic architecture. It has a café and exhibition space and a topographical model of Iceland. The lake itself is home to dozens of ducks and birds. They are described on noticeboards along the footpath that circles the water.

Alongside the lake is **Listasafn Íslands** (National Art Gallery, Fríkirkjuvegur 7; open Tues–Sun 11am–5pm; admission charge, Wed free), a rather cramped place with

Whaling ships, Reykjavík harbour

examples of the work of all Iceland's most famous painters, of whom the best known is probably the pop artist Erró, with the odd Picasso and Munch thrown in for good measure. A couple of blocks away is a very different kind of visual experience, the *Volcano Show* (Hellusund 6a; tel: 551 3230; open daily, July–Aug 10am–9.15pm, Sept–June 3–5.30pm; admission charge). Films are in English, French and German at different times during the day and show dramatic pictures of eruptions, including the one in 1964 that created Iceland's newest island, Surtsey.

The Harbour Area

Just north of the government district are the few streets that lead up to the harbour. These are full of cafés, bars and restaurants and are great for just wandering around. On Tryggvagata is **Hafnarhúsið** (Harbour House Art Museum; open daily 11am–6pm, Thur till 7pm; admission charge, Mon free). Your ticket will also get you into the Kjarvalsstaðir Art Museum and the Ásmundursafn Gallery on the same day (*see pages 33, 34*). The Harbour House is a converted warehouse that contains some extraordinary work by 20th- and 21st-century artists. It can be a little confusing to find your way around, but if you're happy to take pot luck you will come across pieces by the internationally renowned Erró as well as other artists from Iceland and elsewhere.

The **harbour** itself is still fully operational, with fishing boats bringing in their catch. Look out for the five black

whaling ships, each with a red H on its funnel, tied up together. They have been in the harbour since Iceland banned whaling in 1989 under international pressure, and many locals would like to see them put to sea again. There are sometimes visiting restored or replica sailing ships along the piers, and the streets have a variety of tourist shops.

Today's harbour is built on reclaimed land, so you need to go a few streets back to find what used to be the old harbourfront. Here on Hafnarstræti and adjacent Aðalstræti are some of the city's oldest buildings; many of these have been beautifully restored and now house cafés and bars. Café Victor, Hafnarstræti 1–3, for example, was once the **Fálkahúsið**, where the king of Denmark kept his prize falcons. There are two carved wooden falcons on the roof to commemorate the fact. Along the bay to the east is Jón Gunnar Árnason's 1986 sculpture *Sólfar SunCraft,* which is based on a Viking longboat.

Jón Gunnar Árnason's stainless-steel *Sólfar SunCraft*

Western Reykjavík

You will probably arrive into the west of the city, where the bus terminals and domestic airport are situated, but there is little to tempt you out there again before your departure. The exceptions are the normally well-stocked **Þjóðminjasfn Íslands** (National Museum, Hringbraut, junction with Suður-gata; closed for renovation but due to reopen in 2004), and the **Norræna Húsið** (Nordic House, Sturlugata 5; open Tues–Sun noon–5pm; free except for some exhibitions), a Scandinavian cultural centre with a well-stocked library offering free internet access, exhibitions, concerts and a pleasant café.

On the other side of the domestic airport, on a hill known as **Öskjuhlíð**, are six enormous tanks used to store the geo-thermally heated water that supplies the city, as well as a restaurant, a huge artificial geyser and a **viewing platform** (free) with unparalleled views across the city and mountains. At the southern edge of Öskjuhlíð is a beach, **Nauthólsvík** (free), where the seawater is heated by the addition of hot water from the hill. There is a café and a place to hire kayaks, and the Reykjavík Yacht Club is situated alongside.

Eastern Reykjavík

There is more to see on the eastern side of the city. By the sea, isolated on a grassy square, is **Höfði**, often known as the Reagan-Gorbachev House. The building is used as a venue for government receptions and other social functions and hence closed to the public. However, when the two presidents came here in 1986 to discuss cutting nuclear weapons, it helped put Iceland on the international map. You can look through the windows and try to imagine the ghost of a young girl who supposedly haunts the house. She poisoned herself after being found guilty of incest with her brother and is said to spend her time switching on and off lights and knocking pictures off the walls.

Statues beside the city's hot-water tanks on Öskjuhlíð hill

A couple of blocks southwest is **Náttúrufræðisafnið** (Museum of Natural History, Hverfisgata 116; open June–Aug Tues, Thur, Sat, Sun 1–5pm, Sept–May same days 1.30–4pm; admission charge). Its main appeal is for geology and plant enthusiasts, but if you've ever wondered what the Great Auk looked like before it became extinct, you can see a stuffed one here.

Further inland is **Kjarvalsstaðir** (Municipal Gallery, Flókagata; open daily 10am–5pm, Wed 10am–7pm; admission charge except Mon). The building may look an eyesore from the outside, but the exhibits inside are worth the trek. Half the gallery is dedicated to the huge, colourful and often abstract landscapes by the Icelandic artist Jóhannes Kjarval (1885–1972). The other half houses visiting exhibitions.

Look south from here and you should see the imposing domed **Perlan** (Pearl), a revolving restaurant that sits on top of the glistening silver hot-water tanks on Öskjuhlíð hill (*see*

Reykjavík water babies

page 32). The tanks hold 24 million litres (over 5 million gallons) of hot water and cater for almost half of Reykjavík's water consumption. An impressive man-made geyser spewing water at five-minute intervals has been constructed near the 'Pearl', and various efforts over the past two decades to turn Öskjuhlíð into a nature sanctuary have delivered impressive results.

Further east is the **Ásmundursafn** (Asmundur Sveinsson Sculpture Museum, Sigtún; open daily May–Sept 10am–4pm, Oct–Apr 1–4pm; admission charge except Mon), which you can enter on the same ticket as Hafnarhúsið *(see page 30)* and Kjarvalsstaðir *(see page 33)*. This is modern sculpture at its very best, with huge figures depicting the people of Iceland as well as mythical characters. Some good examples are to be found in the wooded garden where you can sit and ponder them even if the museum itself is closed.

A short distance to the east is **Laugardalur**, a huge free park housing a sports stadium, swimming pool, botanical garden and zoo. The gardens feature Icelandic plants as well as large number of imported varieties. There is a children's playground and a duck pond with a replica Viking longboat in it. The **zoo** (open May–Sept daily 10am–6pm; admission charge) is well run and allows the animals plenty of space to run around. You're unlikely to see reindeer or Arctic fox in the wild, so it's well worth taking a look at them here. There are also minx, Icelandic horses, sheep, ducks and seals.

The Outskirts

Just outside Reykjavík there are a number of sights that can be visited on a short bus or taxi journey. To the east is the **Árbæjarsafn** (Arbær Open-Air Museum; open June–Aug Mon 11am–4pm, Tues–Fri 9am–5pm, Sat, Sun 10am–6pm; admission charge.) The original farm was mentioned in the sagas and is now a showcase of how Icelanders used to live. Here, there are old homesteads with turf roofs from all around the country and a church that dates from 1842. The buildings are added to on a regular basis, as the collection expands. There are also exhibitions on the development of public transport and other services in the capital.

To the west is the town of **Hafnarfjörður**, really a suburb of the capital that has developed a major tourist industry of its own. The location is attractive, with parks and cliffs by sea. **Fjörukráin** (Viking Village, Strandgata 50, <www.fjorukrain.is>) houses a guesthouse and two dining areas, one a banqueting hall and the other outside in a Viking camp, with tents and waiters dressed as Vikings. In an old forge is

Smoky Bay's Steamy Power

The name Reykjavík, meaning 'smoky bay', was coined by one of the early settlers who mistook the steam rising from the ground for smoke. Inevitably the arrival of man brought pollution in its wake, especially with the burning of fossil fuels. As the city expanded massively in the 20th century, so did the threat from polluted air. The decision, taken in the 1960s, to convert the city to environmentally friendly power sources cut carbon dioxide emissions from the heating system alone from 270,000 tonnes a year to virtually zero. Today, the geo-thermally heated water that gave the city its name is used to heat its buildings and is even piped beneath the main streets in winter to prevent icing. Reykjavík is arguably the world's greenest capital city.

Reykjavík is increasingly popular as a destination for cruise ships. Almost 30,000 visitors a year come to Iceland this way. The vessels moor in the old port, *Gamla*.

the **Vestnorræntmenning-arsetur** (West Nordic Culture House; open Mon–Fri 1–7pm, Sat, Sun noon–4pm; free), showing handicrafts from Iceland, Greenland and the Faroe Islands. It's all very touristy, and by the time you leave you'll never want to see another horned helmet again.

The town also has a good Museum of Local History, **Sívert-sens-Húsið** (Vesturgata 6; open daily, June–Aug 1–5pm, Sept–May Sat, Sun only 1–5pm; admission charge) and an Institute of Culture and Fine Art, **Hafnarborg** (Strandgata 34; open Wed–Mon noon–6pm; admission charge) with a permanent collection and exhibitions by Icelandic and international artists. There are occasional music recitals and other events.

Just north of the harbour, **Sjóminjasafn Íslands** (Icelandic Maritime Museum; Vesturgata 8; open daily June–Sept 1–5pm, Oct–May Sat, Sun 1–5pm; admission charge) tells not only the history of the town's nautical past, but also has exhibits on some of Iceland's adventurers, notably Leifur Eiríkson who is thought to have reached America long before Columbus. There is a fine church and **sculpture garden** at Viðistaðir on the northern outskirts of the town.

Viðey

Just 1km (½ mile) out to sea due north of Reykjavík is the island of **Viðey**, a small but historically significant place full of old buildings, memorials and grottoes. Just up from the jetty is the oldest building in Iceland, Viðeyjarstofa, built in 1755 and now a classy restaurant. The bird life is prolific on Viðey, and there are some impressive basalt columns on the isthmus at the centre of the island. It's small enough to stroll around with ease in an hour or two. Ferries depart from

Sundahöfn harbour in Reykjavík between June and September (for times, tel: 581 1010), and the trip takes less than 10 minutes. The only puffins to be seen close to the capital are on the tiny island of **Lundey** (*lundi* is Icelandic for puffin). You can't go ashore, but ferries depart from Sundahöfn harbour between June and August for a 2-hour round-the-island trip. Tickets are available from the tourist office at Bankastræti 2.

THE BLUE LAGOON

One trip out of Reykjavík that should not be missed is to the world's greatest outdoor bath, **Bláa Lonið** (Blue Lagoon, Grindavík, tel: 420 8800; open daily 15 May–31 Aug 9am–9pm, 1 Sept–14 May 10am–7.30pm; admission charge). Most hotels will have details of tours, but you can also arrive by public bus. The lagoon is a pool of seawater naturally heated by the geothermal activity below the surface.

Bathing in the Blue Lagoon

It sits in the middle of a lava field and you can lounge around here with warm mud oozing between your toes in water temperatures of 36–39°C (100–110°F) all year round.

The water contains a mixture of salts, silica and blue-green algae, which is said to cleanse and soften the skin and relax the body. The lagoon filled up next to the adjacent Svartsengi power station after its construction in the 1970s. People started to bathe in it and patients with skin complaints reported significant improvements in their condition, so official public bathing facilities were opened in 1987. An outpatients clinic for psoriasis patients was later added.

The facilities have been greatly improved recently, with a new visitors reception and restaurant and a modern shower block. You are now barely aware of the power station. Two saunas have been built alongside the lagoon and for an extra charge you can have a massage and be rubbed with some of the many Blue Lagoon products now on sale in the gift shop. These are said to enhance your energy flow and do wonders for both body and soul.

Whether you believe it all or not, wallowing about in the hot water for an hour or so is a fantastic feeling – and you can spread as much mud over your body as you like for free. Watch out for hot spots in the water, which can be too close to boiling for comfort, but you will come upon them gradually and be able to move away. Take care going down the steps into the lagoon, as they can be slippery and you could have a hard landing on the rocks lurking in the mud under the water. If you are in the lagoon at the end of the day you can watch the sun set while you soak away life's strains. Bathing suits, towels and bath robes can be rented at the reception.

The Blue Lagoon is officially recognised as a psoriasis clinic by the Icelandic Ministry of Health. Patients come from all over the world to soak up its benefits.

Þingvellir, a national park and site of the original parliament

THE GOLDEN CIRCLE

This 200-km (125-mile) round trip from Reykjavík takes in some of the key historical and geological sites in Iceland. They include the original geyser that gave its name to gushing blowholes worldwide, the site of the country's first parliament, and one of its most dramatic waterfalls. You can cover the route on any one of a number of day tours from Reykjavík. They take about seven hours, but include stops at gift shops and eating places along the way. The trip can just about be done by public transport or you could hire a car. The route is well signposted, and parking is good.

Þingvellir

The nearest landmark to the capital on the Golden Circle route is the site of the orginal Alþingi (parliament), established in 930. It is situated in **Þingvellir** (Assembly Plains; admission free), a large national park that has enormous political and geographical significance. Unfortunately, there are few actual monuments or buildings to be seen, and you have to use your imagination to picture the events of the past.

There is a well-marked **information centre** with maps of the area and large boards outside explaining its significance. Fishing and camping permits can be obtained here. It's worth familiarising yourself with the layout of the park before you set off to explore as it's not that well signposted.

The Parliament at Þingvellir

Þingvellir may feel as if it's in the middle of nowhere, but 1,000 years ago it was the focal point of the country. For two weeks every summer Icelanders flooded into the valley to take part in or just watch the proceedings of the Alþingi (parliament). The position was perfect, with plenty of grazing land for horses, good tracks from the more populated parts of Iceland and a lake teeming with fish to feed the multitudes. Trading and socialising went on continuously while the leaders got on with the serious work of running the country. It was the job of the 36 chieftains from the various regions to agree on new laws, under the supervision of the 'lawspeaker'. A Law Council, made up of four regional courts and a supreme court, dealt with infringements and disputes. Huge fines could be imposed and for the most serious crimes the offenders were outlawed from the country, but the system relied on the population to accept its authority voluntarily. It didn't have the power to stop open warfare from breaking out when disputes couldn't be resolved peacefully. From the mid-16th century the courts gained more power, and public executions took place. Men were beheaded, and women convicted of witchcraft or sexual offences were drowned in the river. Alþingi's last meeting was held here in 1798. After that a national court and parliament was established in Reykjavík.

The park is situated on top of the line where the two continental plates of North America and Europe meet. In fact they are slowly moving apart, widening Iceland by 1.5cm (⅝in) a year. From the **Almannagjá viewing point** you can see the rift valley clearly as you look towards the lake. The red-roofed church dates from 1859. It stands on the site of

Hardy Icelandic sheep

a much bigger church that held sway over all the local inhabitants. Below you is the Alþingi site itself. You can walk down into it: a flagpole marks where the leader of the parliament, the law speaker, made his proclamations. Just to the east of the Alþingi the Öxará River flows into a lake, **Þingvallavatn**. There's a 20-m (66-ft) waterfall, and nearby you can clearly see the layers of ash left by successive eruptions.

Skálholt

Next stop on the Golden Circle is **Skálholt**, about 45km (28 miles) to the east of Þingvellir, and a seat of ecclesiastical, rather than political, power. Skálholt was the site of a bishopric from 1056 until a massive earthquake destroyed its cathedral in the late 18th century. The bishop picked up his cassock and headed for the relative safety of Reykjavík, and it wasn't until 1963 that the present church was finally restored and reconsecrated. It's hard to imagine when you see the church that it was once at the centre of the biggest settlement in Iceland and site of the country's first school. Inside you can see the coffin of one of the early bishops, uncovered during the reconstruction work, and a fine modern mosaic

Strokkur in action

above the altar. Alongside the church there is a conference and cultural centre, where concerts and art exhibitions are staged in summer.

Geysir

Another 20km (12 miles) to the northeast you can see evidence of the one power that both church and state have to respect: nature. There are bigger geysers (*geysir* in Icelandic) in the world, and more impressive ones, too, but this is the site of the original. **Geysir** is the one Icelandic word to have made it into the lexicon of world language. Sadly, the gusher that used to shoot 70m (230ft) into the air now does nothing more than gurgle. For years Icelanders poured masses of soap powder into the orifice, a sort of Viagra for geysers, to make it perform, but in the end they gave up. (The English poet W.H. Auden noted in the 1930s that Icelanders were already using imported liquid Sunlight soap – the thinner local type did not work – to encourage Geysir to explode.)

Fortunately, there is the smaller, but more reliable **Strokkur** (literally 'the churn') beside Geysir; Strokkur spurts to a height of around 20m (66ft) every few minutes, without artificial encouragement. Never stand too close to Strokkur – an average of seven tourists are scalded every week during the summer months, mostly from putting their hands in the surrounding water pools to test the temperature.

The whole Geysir area is geothermically active and smells strongly of sulphur (similar to the smell of a rotten egg).

Walking trails are marked out among the steaming vents and glistening, multicoloured mud formations.

Gullfoss

An example of nature at its most forceful is to be found another 6km (4 miles) along the road to the north. **Gullfoss**  (Golden Falls) is, in fact, two separate waterfalls a short distance apart. Their combined drop is 32m (105ft), and the canyon below is some 2km (just over a mile) long, with basalt columns like the pipes of an organ rising up from the bottom. Trails climb past the waterfall's northern face, allowing you to get within an arm's length of the awesome flow. Wear a raincoat, or the clouds of spray that create photogenic rainbows on sunny days will douse you from head to foot. The falls were nearly destroyed by a hydroelectric dam project in the 1920s, but now the area is protected.

Gullfoss carving out a canyon

THE WESTMAN ISLANDS

The Westman Islands, or *Vestmannaeyjar* to give them their Icelandic name, are a long strip of 15 islands and numerous rocks about 10km (6 miles) off the south coast of Iceland. Carbon dating has suggested that they may have been the first part of the country to be inhabited. They were created by underwater eruptions, and the process is still ongoing: the newest island, Surtsey, emerged from the sea as recently as the mid-1960s. It has been studied with fascination by scientists, not just because of its dramatic appearance, but for the flora and fauna that are taking root and making it their home.

The tourist authorities describe the islands as the 'Capri of the North', although even they wouldn't claim it was anything to do with the weather. The coves and inlets may be reminiscent of the chic Italian island, but the rain and wind

The Westman Islands, the earliest inhabited part of Iceland

that batter them for much of the year certainly are not.

Heimaey

The only inhabited island is **Heimaey**, which can be reached by ferry or plane, although low cloud can close the airport at short notice. It has a pretty little town, but most visitors come for the surrounding countryside and **bird cliffs**.

Molten lava

Hundreds of thousands of puffins, as well as guillemots, fulmars and 30 other types of seabird come here every year to nest and breed on the precipitous cliffs. You can reach them on foot or take a boat out and get a better view from the sea. You might also see whales and seals in the waters around the islands. (Keikó, the killer whale that starred in the Hollywood film *Free Willy* lived in the harbour here for a few years after a public campaign in the US to have him returned to the wild. He's since moved on to Norway.)

The other big draw of Heimaey is the landscape. Two dramatic cones rise up just outside the town: the volcano, Helgafell, and a much newer mountain, Eldfell, created in a massive eruption in 1973 that almost buried the town. In the early hours of 23 January 1973 a fissure nearly 2-km (1-mile) long opened up on the eastern side of Helgafell. Red hot lava started to spurt into the sky heralding an eruption that was to last for the next six months. The threat to the town was immediate and the entire 5,000-strong population was taken off to the mainland. Flying bombs of molten lava crashed through windows or melted through roofs, and a colossal river of lava made its way towards the town. Many houses collapsed under the weight of falling ash and by the time the flow stopped a quarter of Heimaey had been destroyed. The harbour was saved at the last minute and to this day nobody is sure whether this was just luck or whether the millions of tons of seawater that the emergency services poured onto the advancing river of rock did the trick. Either way the harbour had a new wall and much better protection from the elements. When it was all over the island was 2.2 sq km (½ sq mile) larger, and the new mountain of Eldfell had been created. You can see a film, the *Volcano Show*, that includes some dramatic footage of the eruption daily in the town centre in summer.

Around the island there are numerous walks, the best of which is off to the west coast and the valley of Herjólfsdalur. Venture a little further and you will reach some of the best bird cliffs, where you can get remarkably close to the puffins.

The Westman Islanders are great sports enthusiasts. There are four football fields on the islands and a modern sports centre with a pool. You can easily take in some fishing, rock climbing or golf if you stay for long enough.

Puffins

The puffin is a national symbol in Iceland as well as a national dish. It is a member of the auk family and has a multicoloured beak and bright orange legs and feet. Puffins are highly sociable, often standing about in groups and nesting in large colonies. They fish together, too, forming wide rafts out to sea. They can dive to 60m (200ft) in search of fish, but also eat plankton in winter. They rarely travel far from their colony while raising their young. Both parents incubate a single egg. The males and females look very similar, but neither grow much more than 30cm (12in) in height. They produce a dark meat, like duck but less fatty, which is often served with a fruity sauce.

The puffin is Iceland's national symbol

THE SOUTH COAST

The stretch of highway that runs east along the south of Iceland is a mixture of long, almost featureless lava fields and wonderful views of the mountain and glaciers that come down to the sea in the southeast. It has a reputation as the wettest part of the country, but if the weather holds it is also one of the most dramatic. This is also one of the many regions to see and ride Icelandic horses *(see What To Do)*.

As you leave Reykjavík and pass Selfoss, heading east, look out for **Mt Hekla**. On a fine day its cone provides a perfect backdrop to Reykjavík, but it's frequently shrouded in cloud. It's an active volcano that has wiped out farming in the surrounding area several times and erupted every 10 years or so since 1970; however, it can still be climbed fairly easily. Discover route details and background history at **Heklumið-stöðin** (Hekla Museum; open June–Aug daily 10am–6pm; admission charge), at Leirubakki farm on route 26.

Þórsmörk

You are now entering saga country and, in particular, the setting for the most bloody of the sagas – that which tells the story of the wise and decent Njál and the gruesome end that met most of his friends and family. Much of the action took place at the Alþingi at Þingvellir *(see page 40)*, but there was more than a little blood-letting near the village of Hvolsvöllur where there is now an Icelandic Saga Centre with background information on the various tales. Here, there is a turning northeast to **Þórsmörk**, a beautiful valley that is well worth the detour. City dwellers from Reykjavík flock here at weekends to enjoy the wooded walks, flora and fauna and lovely views.

East of Þórsmörk is **Skógar**, home to a meticulously managed folk museum (open daily summer 9am–7pm), the most visited of its kind in Iceland. In addition to a 6,000-piece collection, the museum has examples of different types of Icelandic housing through the ages.

There is a summer Edda Hotel at Skógar, as well as the splendid waterfall, Skógafoss, the sheer fall of which offers one of south Iceland's best photo opportunities. The trek

Skógar homestead

from here to Þórsmörk, passing between the ice-caps of Eyjafjallajökull and Myrdalsjökull over the Fimmvörðuháls pass, is popular with the hardy between June and September, so much so that it becomes quite crowded, particularly in July. There are two huts between the ice-caps: one is an emergency shelter; the other is pre-bookable.

Seljalandsfoss tumbles down the cliff-face

Vík

Continuing east, the next major stop is the coastal town of **Vík**, or, to give it its full name, Vík í Mýrdal (Bay of the Marshy Valley). It's a pretty little town whose symbol of a smiling yellow face greets you everywhere, possibly to try to counter its reputation as the rainiest place in Iceland. Most people come here for the black volcanic sand, cliffs and birdlife. Three steeples of stone, known as **Reynisdrangar** ◀ (Troll Rocks), rise out of the sea. Legend has it they are the figures of trolls that turned to stone when they failed to get under cover before the sun hit them. Whatever their origin, they teem with birdlife in summer. There are kittiwakes, Arctic tern, puffins, gannets and guillemots in the vicinity.

The road crosses more barren fields of lava and *sandur*, a mix of silt, sand and gravel. Oddly shaped boulders are partly overgrown with lichens, helping to give the area a somewhat other-worldly feel. Little wooden bridges cross the rivers,

Reynisdrangar (Troll Rocks)

reducing the highway to one lane. In the middle of all this is the tiny hamlet of **Kirkjubæjarklaustur**, a good place to pick up provisions. While doing so, you can reflect on the power of prayer, for it was here that the local pastor delivered his 'Fire Sermon', which believers will tell you halted the flow of lava during the Lakagígar eruption of 1783 and saved the church. A memorial chapel, built in 1974, commemorates the miracle.

A rough road, which is accessible only to four-wheel-drive vehicles, goes from Kirkjubæjarklaustur to the **Lakagígar Crater Row**, where you can see some of the effects of the 1783 eruptions that lasted for 10 months and were known as the Skaftáreldar (Skaftá river fires). The eruption was the largest recorded in the world, and the lava produced was equivalent to 12 cubic km (7½ cubic miles). Most of Iceland's livestock died from the poisonous fumes. Some 100 craters extend for 25km (15 miles) up to the glacier; the surrounding lava field is dotted with caves and other lava formations. It takes several hours to see them properly, but there are amazing views from the top of Laki itself – a climb of about an hour.

Vatnajökull

The massive **Vatnajökull**, the biggest ice-cap in Europe, is almost 150km (90 miles) across and dominates the south-eastern corner of Iceland. Driving around the ring road you can get fascinating glimpses of it as it breaks through the mountains. To get close to the ice-cap, though, you have to leave the main road and head inland. Its size and beauty, however, is best appreciated from the air, particularly on an internal flight from Reykjavík to Egilsstaðir or Höfn.

In October 1996 Vatnajökull was besieged by the world's media when a fissure 4km (2½ miles) long opened beneath the surface of the glacier. Within two days a 10-km (6-mile) column of steam was rising above the ice. Massive flooding was predicted, but the eruption fizzled out, and the journalists departed. Then, on 5 November, the ice dam broke and a huge surge of water burst forth, destroying bridges and roads and carrying massive ice blocks with it.

A number of smaller valley glaciers, all linked to Vatnajökull, are most clearly visible from the road. One of these, Skaftafellsjökull, stops close to the **Skaftafell National Park** (information office open daily May–Sept 8am–9pm). In the

The immense Vatnajökull ice-cap

shadow of Iceland's highest peak, **Hvannadalshnúkur** (2,120m/6,950ft), this is serious walking territory and very popular in summer. But with so many trails into the hills, it's not difficult to find solitude. Hikers take day-long round trips to the higher moorlands and peaks, such as those at **Kristínartindur**. Among the shorter walks is the route up to **Svartifoss** (Black Falls), named after the surrounding sombre cliffs of basalt.

Jökulsárlón

Continuing east, the next major point of interest is the extraordinary glacier river lagoon at **Jökulsárlón**. This photogenic

Icebergs in Jökulsárlón

spot is just off the road where a small bridge crosses the mouth of the lake. Here great slabs of ice that have broken off the **Breiðamerkur-jökull** valley glacier float eerily in the water. The icebergs, some of which are as big as houses, shimmer with a translucent blue as the light catches them. For a fee (summer only), you can take a ride in a dinghy and see the icebergs at close quarters; your guide may even pull a 1,000-year old piece of ice out of the water for you to admire.

The glacial lagoon was the dramatic backdrop to scenes in two James Bond films, *A View to a Kill* and *Die Another Day*.

Höfn

The final outpost in southeastern Iceland is the town of **Höfn**, which translates simply as 'harbour'. If you are heading for the Eastfjords *(see page 74)* by public transport you might find yourself having to stay overnight here. It's not the most exciting of places, unless you fancy examining the fish-freezing plant. However, if the skies are clear, there are good views back over the glacier. Tours of the glacier by four-wheel drive can be organised, but if your budget doesn't stretch to that, there is an exhibition adjacent to the tourist office (Hafnarbraut 25; open daily mid-May–mid-Sept 8am–8pm; free) telling you all you need to know about glaciers .

Hvítserkur, a basalt stack flecked with guano

THE NORTH COAST

If you are restricted to one part of the country in addition
to the Reykjavík area, there is a good chance you will
choose the north coast. It's the most accessible region to
reach and, in many ways, the liveliest. Akureyri is generally
considered to be the capital of the north, and Húsavík is the
best point of departure in Iceland for whale-watching.

Despite being close to the Arctic Circle, the north also has
the best weather, and temperatures can reach a balmy 20°C
(68°F) or more in summer. The coastline is very dramatic
in places, and there are some huge fjords – a feature that is
almost completely lacking in the south.

Akureyri
Whether you fly, drive or take a bus you are almost certain to
end up in **Akureyri**, and it's a town well worth spending

some time in. It's an attractive place and has a lot more life about it than most provincial towns. It is home to the only professional theatre in Iceland outside the capital, for example, as well as the only university. Many parts of the country suffer from an exodus of young people, but not Akureyri, which has a youthful feel about it. Since the late 1990s the restaurants and bars have become increasingly fashionable. In summer the town is busy with tourists and in winter it's a major destination for conferences.

Akureyri is surrounded by high mountains, which are up to 1,500m (5,000ft) tall and snowcapped for much of the year. Green and lush in comparison to many other towns, it even has its own forest and a golf course (every June the Arctic Open tees off under the midnight sun). Akureyri is also a good starting point for visiting some of the most beautiful parts of the country, both to the east and the west.

The centre of town is compact. The main shopping street is the pedestrianised **Hafnarstræti**. It runs from close to the huge main church *(see below)* towards the rather nondescript town square, Ráðhústorg. Running east from the square is Strandgata, which has become the trendy corner of town; this leads down to the port, where cruise liners dock in summer.

The church steeples of the **Akureyrarkirkja** (open daily 10am–noon, 2–4pm; free) tower over the town and are most dramatic at night when spotlit against the dark sky. The church was designed by the architect Guðjón Samúelsson, who was also responsible for

Akureyrarkirkja at night

the vast Hallgrímskirkja in Reykjavík *(see page 25)*. Inside is a fine stained-glass window from the original cathedral at Coventry in the English Midlands. The window was removed at the start of World War II before the cathedral was destroyed by bombs; it was rescued from a London antiques shop and now forms the centrepiece of an impressive display that also features scenes from Iceland's own history.

Having clambered up to the church there is a gentler climb to another of the town's main attractions, the **Lystigarðurinn** (Botanical Gardens; Eyrarlandsvegur; open June–Oct Mon–Fri 8am–10pm, Sat, Sun 9am–10pm; free). It's a tribute to the milder weather in this part of Iceland that so many species from all around the world are able to survive in the open air. The gardens have been here since 1912, when they were started by a Danish woman to provide a relaxing atmosphere for families, but the flower collection dates from the mid-1950s. There are species from southern Europe, Africa, South America and Australasia, as well as examples of just about every variety that grows in Iceland. The gardens are very well kept, and their original purpose – as a haven of calm – still thrives today.

The Botanical Gardens

If you want a bit of fauna to go with the flora, the **Náttúrufræðustifnun** (Natural History Museum; Hafnarstræti 81; open daily June–Sept 10am–5pm; admission charge) has a complete set of stuffed Icelandic birds and their eggs as well as mammals and fish.

The excellent **Ainjasafnið a Akureyri** (Akureyri Municipal Museum; Aðalstræti

View across the rooftops of Akureyri

58; open daily June–mid-Sept 11am–5pm, mid-Sept–May 2–4pm; admission charge) has a wide collection of everyday items that date as far back as the settlement in the 9th century, including a beautifully painted pulpit. The church here is still used for weddings. **Listasafn Akureyrar** (Kaupvangsstræti 24; open Tues–Sun 2–6pm, Fri, Sat till 10pm; free) is the town's Art Gallery and shows off the talents of a wide range of local painters as well as hosting international exhibitions in the summer. Some artists have studios attached to the gallery, and there is an art school, too.

The town's **swimming pool** (Þingvallastræti 2; open daily 1–9pm; admission charge) is one of the best in the country, with facilities including a waterslide, hot tubs, a steam room and sauna. Attached is a family park with mini-golf, electric cars and other distractions for children.

An hour's walk south of the town is a recently planted forest at **Kjarnaskógur**. Given the shortage of trees in Iceland

Iceland's tallest man, Jóhann Kristinn Pétursson, known as Jóhann the Giant, was an impressive 2.34m (7ft 7in) tall. Born in 1913, he worked in circuses and shows in Europe and the US. He returned to Dalvík late in his life and died there in 1984.

this is considered something of an attraction, and the townspeople flock here on sunny weekends. There is a children's play area, picnic sites and a jogging track.

Eyjafjörður

From Akureyri two roads fork off to the north along each side of Eyjafjörður fjord. The cluster of towns and villages on the banks of the fjord are hemmed in close to the water by high mountains. The land here is particularly fertile, and the mild climate makes it good farming territory. It's a suitable area for exploring both on land and at sea, with ferry links to the islands of Grímsey and Hrísey.

Dalvík, a fishing village about an hour's drive north of Akureyri, is the main centre on this side of the fjord. The town was rebuilt after an earthquake in 1934 demolished half the buildings, but the harbourfront is still attractive. The town has a good outdoor swimming pool and an interesting museum, **Byggðasafnið Hvoll** (Karlsbraut; open daily June–mid-Sept 1–5pm; admission charge), in the house of Iceland's tallest man, Jóhann Kristinn Pétursson (see box above). It contains photographs of him and many of his possessions as well as examples of local wildlife, including a stuffed polar bear.

From Dalvík you can catch a ferry to the island of **Grímsey**. The Arctic Circle runs through the centre of this island, and you can get a certificate for crossing it. The small settlement of **Sandvík** has some basic services, including a swimming pool. The community centre commemorates the island's benefactor, Daniel Willard Fiske, a 19th-century

American chess champion who had read about its reputation for producing great chess players since Viking days. He left money for a school and library to be built and donated 11 marble chess boards. The locals still celebrate his birthday on 11 November although, a little ungratefully, hardly any of them play chess any more.

Most visitors come to Grímsey for the extensive **birdlife** – the craggy cliffs on the north and east of the island are home to about 60 species, including puffins, kittiwakes and razorbills. You can explore on your own or find a local guide in the town. The only proper road runs along the west side of Grímsey from Sandvík to the airport, from where there are regular flights to Akureyri. The runway has to be regularly cleared of birds, and this is sometimes done by incoming flights buzzing the airstrip before coming round again to land.

From Árskógssandur, just south of Dalvík, a ferry departs every hour for the 15-minute trip out to the island of **Hrísey**, another choice destination for bird lovers. In particular, the island is a haven for the fearless ptarmigan; they are prolific all year round, although their number swells in the autumn, and they can often be seen waddling down the streets. There are almost 40 species of birds on the island, and it is an important breeding ground for both eider duck and the Arctic tern.

Golden plover

On the eastern side of the fjord the first place of interest is the fishing village of **Svalbarðseyri**. According to local folklore, this is home to a large community of elves who live in the cliffs behind the village.

Church interior, Þingeyrar

Even if this sounds all rather unlikely, you are still sure to be enchanted here – by the rugged coastline.

At **Laufás**, some 30km (19 miles) to the north of Akureyri, there is a magnificent example of a 19th-century turf farmhouse, maintained by the Icelandic National Museum (open daily June–mid-Sept 10am– 6pm; admission charge). The herringbone design of turf on the walls is superbly preserved. Inside there is a multitude of effects showing how life was lived here more than 100 years ago. The timber church dates from 1865.

West of Akureyri

On the route west, the tiny village of **Hófsós** is home to **Vesturfarasetrið** (Icelandic Emigration Centre; open daily June–Aug 11am–6pm; admission charge). If you think you are of Icelandic descent, this is the place to come to try and trace your roots. There is a good exhibition telling the story of those Icelanders who emigrated west to the US and Canada. Next door is a well-preserved traditional warehouse made from Danish imported timber in 1777. Inside is a bizarre collection of devices for trapping birds.

Hólar í Hjaltadal, located 25km (15 miles) to the southeast and inland from the coast road, was once a thriving cultural and religious centre. Until the Reformation it was a great seat of learning, with monks studying the scriptures and transcribing manuscripts. It housed the country's first printing press, dating from 1530. But all that has gone, and it's now a quiet and peaceful place. A red-stone **cathedral** (ask at the neighbouring college for entry), dating from 1759–63, commemorates its religious past. There is sacred art and sculpture on display as well as a modern mosaic by the artist Erró. The bones of the last Catholic bishop in Iceland, Jón Arason, are buried here. He was beheaded in 1550 for resisting the spread of the protestant Reformation.

Among the most important historical sites in Iceland is **Þingeyrar**, 85km (53 miles) further west. It was the home of one of the first regional assemblies as well as the first monastery in 1133. It was here that many of the sagas were written, and other texts were transcribed by the monks. The monastery disappeared after the Reformation, but there is an impressive 19th-century church, **Þingeyrarkirkja**, made of basalt, that is visible for miles around. The interior has a

Þingeyrarkirkja, built of basalt blocks transported on sledges

On the look-out for whales

dramatic blue ceiling with 1,000 gold stars painted on it, white walls and green pews. The altarpiece, which was made in Nottingham, England, came from the old monastery.

Húsavík

To the northeast of Akureyri, **Húsavík** occupies a beautiful setting, nestled among high cliffs and facing out over the Arctic. Not surprisingly the sea has always been a dominant factor in the town's development, and today people flock here for **whale-watching tours**, for which Húsavík is renowned.

Down at the harbour is the **Whale Centre** (open daily June–Sept 9am–9pm; admission charge), Iceland's only museum dedicated to these captivating mammals. It contains photographs, models and skeletons to help explain the life-cycle, habits and biology of whales. If you are interested in some of the sea's smaller inhabitants, and how they find their way on to our dinner plates, the centre will also organise visits to the nearby fish processing factory. Húsavík also has an excellent natural history museum, **Safnahúsið**, (Stóri-garður 17; open daily June–Aug 10am–6pm; admission charge) in the same building as the town library. As well as memorabilia from old houses and farms, there is a recon-struction of a Viking longboat, various old weapons, exhibits of flora and fauna and, the item of which they are most proud,

Whales and Whaling

For many visitors, Iceland's attitude to whaling is perplexing. In almost every other way the country has a magnificent record for envi-ronmental protection and respect for nature. Yet the vast majority of Icelanders support a return to commercial whaling, almost as a badge of national pride. The only thing that stops them is the fear of crip-pling economic sanctions from the rest of the world.

The abundance of whales off Iceland's coasts led inevitably to them being caught and killed for food. In 1948 this developed into a commercial whaling industry that continued until 1989. In less-sensitive days tourists would go out of their way to watch whales being sliced up in the open air, but more recently views have hardened.

Keikó, the killer whale who starred in the Hollywood film *Free Willy*, came to live in Iceland in 1998 after a campaign in the US to have him restored to his natural habitat. He improved the country's reputation as whale-friendly for a while, although he has since moved on to Norway.

In March 1999 the Icelandic parliament voted by a large majority to resume commercial whaling, but so far only a research project into the likely economic implications has been launched. So, for the moment, Icelandic boats take to the waters to spot whales rather than hunt them. The most common are the medium-sized minke whales, which are seen on most trips, as well as humpbacks, which can be as long as 15m (50ft), and fin whales. Blue whales, orcas and sperm whales are sometimes seen, as are dolphins and porpoises.

a stuffed polar bear captured on the island of Grímsey in 1969. A new maritime museum was added in 2002, with a broad range of exhibits reflecting the town's historical dependence on the sea. The library offers free Internet access.

The **church** (Garðarsbraut; open daily June–Aug 9am–noon, 1–5pm; free), an impressive wooden building in the shape of a cross, was built in 1906–7 to seat 450 people. The altarpiece features several of the town's residents who posed for a depiction of the resurrection of Lazarus.

There is a well-kept park alongside the river, with a duck-pond attracting long-tailed squaws and eiders. On the southern edge of the town there is a nine-hole golf course, while further south are two man-made warm lagoons, one of which offers free trout fishing.

Boat trips from the harbour go out to two small islands: **Lundey** (Puffin Island) and **Flatey** (Flat Island). Don't be confused, there's another, much more interesting, Flatey off the west coast *(see page 81)*.

East of Húsavík, **Þórshöfn** is another place that dates back to the saga times. It grew considerably in the early 20th century during the peak of the herring boom and is still predominantly a fishing town.

Húsavík harbour

Britain's Prince Charles used to favour **Vopnafjörður**, 60km (37 miles) to the southeast, for fishing holidays. He must have arrived by air, as the roads around here are among the worst in Iceland. The locals will tell you that Santa Claus lives on the nearby **Smjörfjöll** – at least he is able to travel freely by sleigh.

Lake Mývatn, at the centre of a volcanically active region

LAKES, VOLCANOES, CANYONS AND FALLS

Within easy striking distance of both Akureyri and Húsavík are some of the most impressive geological formations in Iceland. These include two massive waterfalls, Dettifoss and Goðafoss, and Jökulsárgljúfur National Park *(see page 71)* which encloses a spectacular canyon with falls of its own. Lake Mývatn, home to a huge variety of ducks, is surrounded by active geothermal areas, craters and bizarre rock formations. A good road circles the lake close to the shore.

The perfectly proportioned falls at **Goðafoss** are easily reached on the drive into the area from the north. The 'Waterfall of the Gods' was so-named because it was here in the year 1000 that the law-speaker Þorgeir decided Iceland should convert to Christianity before throwing his pagan carvings into the waters.

Although small, **Reykjahlíð**, at the northeast corner of Lake Mývatn, is nonetheless the best place to base yourself,

Reykjahlíð church

and tours of the surrounding area can easily be organised from here. The main sight in the village is its **church**, which is surrounded by hardened lava. A major eruption in 1729 brought lava streaming down from the hills. While it obliterated nearby farmland, it skirted around the church. Tradition says it was the power of prayer that protected it, although the walls around the cemetery may have helped. There is a carving on the pulpit depicting the more religious explanation.

Lake Mývatn

Despite its name, **Lake Mývatn** (Midge Lake) is one of the highlights of a visit to Iceland. Midges and flies love the shallow water at the lake's edge, but they rarely bite and you can get a hat with netting attached to keep them out of eyes, ears and mouth. The lake, and the **Laxá River** that flows out from the west, are renowned for the variety of **birds** they attract. The area is protected by law, and there are wardens to help visitors enjoy themselves without harming the ecology.

With the peaks of the Krafla volcano and Mt Hverfjall as a backdrop, Lake Mývatn has a serenity that belies the churning geothermal activity just below the surface of the surrounding land. Only the gently rising columns of steam give away the fact that this is a highly active volcanic region. Around the lake's shore horses and sheep graze quietly, and fishermen patiently wait for trout and Arctic char to bite.

The land around the shore is generally flat, with just a few small hills and mini-craters, making it ideal territory for gentle hiking. The Nature Conservation Agency publishes a list of suggested trails. It's worth carrying binoculars because, whether you are an avid birdwatcher or not, the number and variety of **ducks** and other birdlife here is extraordinary *(see box)*.

At the southern end of the lake, **Skútustaðir** has a couple of hotels and facilities for horseriding and hiring bikes. Close to the shore there is a collection of **pseudocraters**, which look almost like mini-volcanoes. In fact they were created when molten lava ran over the marshland. The water below came to the boil and burst through the lava sheet to

The Ducks and Birds of Mývatn

According to Iceland's Nature Conservation Agency, more species of ducks are believed to inhabit Lake Mývatn and the Laxá River than anywhere else in the world. Along with geese, swans and other birds, there are tens of thousands of these birds, all attracted by the shallow water, plentiful food and space for nesting.

The most common varities are the tufted duck, scaup, wigeon, teal and red-breasted merganser. Harlequin ducks live on the rivers in large numbers, and the common scooter, a diving breed, is widely seen on the west side of the lake. Some rare breeds bring ornithologists to Lake Mývatn from all over the world. The barrow's goldeneye is only found here and in North America, for example. In the Rockies, where the species originates, these birds lay their eggs in holes in tree trunks; here, they lay them in holes in the lava. The Slavonian grebe builds floating nests close to the shore. The gadwall and red-necked phalarope are common all over the lake.

Other breeds you are likely to see include whooper swans, greylag geese, Arctic tern and the black-headed gull. Ptarmigans are common, and there are several pairs of gyrfalcon nesting here, along with smaller numbers of short-eared owl and merlin.

form cones. Most of the islands in the middle of the lake were formed in the same way.

The Laxá River contains salmon, brown trout and Arctic char, but you'll need to buy a licence if you want to fish. Further north is the peak of **Vindbelgjarfjall** (530m/1,735ft), which can be climbed by a fairly steep path at the back of the mountain for some fantastic views. From here, the road passes through wetlands containing some of the biggest concentrations of birdlife, before returning to Reykjahlíð.

Geothermal Sites

There is plenty of evidence to indicate just how close the geothermal activity is to the surface in this part of Iceland – you may well see gases rising from fissures in the lava around Reykjahlíð. The local swimming pool here is naturally heated, and there are numerous ovens for baking bread in the hot earth or for smoking fish using dried sheep dung. You can try both at the local restaurants.

On the southern edge of town the hot springs at **Storagjá** can be reached via a ladder and rope. Unfortunately, they have cooled in recent years and become infested with algae, which disuades most potential swimmers from taking the

> The local tradition of underground baking involves mixing rye dough with yeast and molasses, pouring the mixture into old milk cartons and baking them in holes covered by metal sheets for a day. The result is a heavy but moist steam bread known as *hverabrauð*.

plunge. Another pool, **Grótagjá**, on the Egilsstaðir road, suffers from the opposite problem – it's too hot for most people, but is well worth a look as it's inside a naturally formed cavern in the lava.

Continuing in the same direction is a natural **sauna** in a rather scruffy-looking hut that is welcoming and

Viti crater, on the side of the Krafla volcano

has been free to all-comers for years. The **diatomite plant** at Bjarnarflag shows all this natural energy being put to practical use. The steam is used to clean impurities from the microscopic fossils that are used to make the filtering agent. There are steaming bore holes in the area, and one of the largest underground bakeries is nearby, where you can peek at the slowly baking loaves.

A road off to the north takes you up towards the **Krafla volcano**. There have been eruptions in and around Krafla for much of the past 3,000 years. The so-called Krafla Fires of 1977–84 left a huge field of lava that is still steaming today. The eruption threatened the **Leirbotn power station**, but stopped just short and you can visit the plant for free most afternoons. Further up the road is a perfectly rounded crater **Viti** ('Hell'), which was formed in 1724 and has since flooded. Its huge size, the strange blue tint to the water and the sheer drop down from the rim makes it an awesome

Dettifoss, a raging torrent in Jökulsárgljúfur National Park

sight. From the Krafla car park you can visit a second crater, **Sjálfskapar Viti**, or 'Home-made Hell', so-called because it was formed when a borehole being drilled for the power station exploded. Fortunately, nobody was killed, but debris from the rig was found for miles around. A well-marked track leads up to the **Leirhnjúkur crater** and the **Krafla Caldera**, formed in the mid-18th century and now a colourful collection of bubbling mud-holes encrusted with sulphur. You can walk around them, but stick to the well-worn paths. Note that the lighter coloured soil is thin and could give way under a person's weight.

Close to the eastern edge of Lake Mývatn is the enchanting **Dimmuborgir basin**. This is another of those places with two histories, one based on folklore, the other on geology. The more romantic account tells that a group of Icelandic trolls were partying here late at night and having such fun that they didn't notice the time; they danced until dawn when the sun turned them all to stone. The more earthy explanation is that lava flowed into a lake here until the basin edge gave way and it gradually drained off leaving pillars of rock behind that had been formed by steam rising through the molten lava. Either way, the basin contains a maze of weirdly shaped arches, caves and other formations. You have to keep to the paths to protect the rock from damage, but it's a lovely spot to explore.

Jökulsárgljúfur National Park

North of Mývatn, **Jökulsárgljúfur National Park** straddles part of Iceland's second-longest river, the **Jökulsá á Fjöllum**. More than half the country's plant species are to be found here, but most visitors are drawn by the geology of the area.

Jökulsárgljúfur itself is a vast canyon up to 120m (395ft) deep and 500m (1,640ft) wide, and its name means 'glacier river canyon'. There are numerous waterfalls along its route. The two most impressive of them, **Dettifoss** (Europe's most powerful falls) and **Selfoss**, are situated at the southern boundary of the park. At the northern tip is the information office where you can acquire details of the area's many walking trails and sights.

From the tourist office a road leads down towards the **Ásbyrgi canyon**, a 90-m (295-ft) semicircle of rock flecked with colourful lichens. The first Viking settlers believed the canyon was formed by Sleipnir, the god Odin's flying horse, crashing a giant hoof into the earth. There are three campsites in the park if you want to stay and explore.

> The Arctic tern is nature's own dive-bomber. If disturbed, it flies down from a great height and attacks while squawking furiously. The best way to ward off the terns is to walk around with a clenched fist or newspaper held up above your head.

Fjord on Iceland's east coast

EASTERN ICELAND

The eastern part of Iceland is one of the least-visited areas of the country and, as a result, has a less well-developed tourist industry. There is not as much volcanic activity here as in some areas of the island, and overall the region has a quiet, gentle feel, making it pleasant to visit. Other advantages for the tourist include the fairer weather – the east is generally warmer and sunnier in summer than other parts of Iceland – and the undulating farmland and rugged coast are ideal for walking.

Plans to build a huge dam and aluminium plant in the eastern highlands have been hugely controversial. Although the area, around Kárahnúkar, is remote and little visited, environmentalists led by the Icelandic Nature Conservation Association say that the impact of the project will be catastrophic. In 2003, however, it looked very likely that the government and the Alcoa company would go ahead with the project.

Egilsstaðir

With its airport and its pivotal position on the ring road, **Egilsstaðir** is the most-visited town in the region. It's not the loveliest of places, but it's a good base for trips to the lakes and mountains to the south of it. There is a modern concrete **church**, designed to reflect the surrounding mountains, and the excellent **Minjasafn Austurlands** (East Iceland Heritage Museum, Tjarnabraut; open June–Aug Tues–Sun 11am–5pm; admission charge). It's packed with all manner of crafts and folklore exhibits and has an indoor turf farmhouse, no bigger than a large shed, that was inhabited until 1964. Also on show is a slightly ghoulish skeleton of a man excavated from a Viking grave in 1995.

The town has a good-sized **swimming pool**, which is ideal for relaxing in after a day's walking.

Lögurinn and Snæfell

The lake of **Lögurinn** runs 30km (19 miles) south from Egilsstaðir, carrying the **Largarfljót River** from the Vatnajökull ice-cap to the sea. The road around it is rough in places, but, unusually for Iceland, the banks are forested, especially on the eastern side. The lake is in a deep glacial valley and is said to be home to the **Lagarfljótsormur monster**, a creature not unlike Scotland's Loch Ness monster, although nobody seems to have got close enough to be sure.

The forest at **Hallormsstaður** is the showcase for Iceland's efforts at re-forestation after the indiscriminate

According to folklore, a young girl found a gold ring and put it in a box with a small snake for safekeeping. When she returned both the ring and snake had grown. Terrified, she threw them into Lögurinn. The snake grew into the Lagarfljótsormur monster, threatening all who crossed the lake.

felling of previous eras. The **arboretum** has examples of many native and imported trees, all of which are well labelled. There are marked trails here for hikes or horseriding.

At 1,833m (6,012ft), **Mt Snæfell** is Iceland's highest peak outside the glacial zones. Although it last erupted some 10,000 years ago, geologists believe that it's still technically active. There are marker posts up the western side of the mountain showing the easiest route to the top, although you need to be experienced to tackle the peak itself. However, there are plenty of easier walks on the mountain, and there is the added attraction of the many reindeer that inhabit the area.

Hardy reindeer grazing on Mt Snæfell

The Eastfjords

Although the inlets along the east of Iceland are less dramatic than those in the west and north, they are dotted with lovely little villages, most of which are easily accessible from the ring road. Travellers arriving in Iceland by ferry normally dock at **Seyðisfjörður**, a pretty little port surrounded by high mountains. A dirt road up to Mt Bjófur gives spectacular views down over the town and the fjord. The harbour area and Old Town, with its brightly painted wooden houses, is a good spot simply to wander. The town's **Bláa kirkjan** (Blue Church) organises classical concerts on Wednesday evenings, and on the same day (the day the ferry leaves) there is a craft market in town.

From **Neskaupstaður**, Iceland's easternmost settlement, **cruises** can be taken to see some of the neighbouring fjords, and perhaps whales and seals as well.

Cheery Icelander

Eskifjörður is a busy fishing village with a large trawler fleet and a fish-freezing plant. **Sjóminjasafn** (Maritime Museum; open daily mid-June–Aug 2–5pm; admission charge) is packed with boats, models, nets and fishing equipment. Just south of here, on a tall headland, is the **Hólmaborgir nature reserve**, where there are easy walks up to the summit.

The hills around the small fishing port of **Reyðarfjörður** have been worn flat by the now-vanished glaciers. The town was a naval base in World War II, and there is a museum, **Stríðsáasafnið** (Austurvegur; open daily mid-June–Aug 1–5pm; admission charge), which tells the story of Iceland's involvement in the war through photographs and other exhibits. In the town's historic streets, fishermen promenade on fine days, and plants are neatly lined up in the windows of corrugated-iron buildings.

A trip out from **Djúpivogur** to the island of **Papey**, 'Monk's Island', reveals Iceland's smallest church – little bigger than a hen coop – and a massive **puffin colony**. The island is thought to have been inhabited by Irish monks until they were frightened off by the arrival of the Vikings.

THE WEST FJORDS

The shocking state of many of the roads and the often-inhospitable climate mean that the West Fjords is a relatively little-visited part of Iceland. However, if you have sufficient time and stamina you can discover one of the real highlights of the country. Inland it's incredibly rugged, and the road wiggles around the narrow strip of flat land between the craggy fjords and the mountains.

Ísafjörður and Around

The only town of any real size in the region is **Ísafjörður**. The deep harbour has helped it to become a major trading centre as well as an important fishing community. For a taste of just how tough an industry it can be, visit the **West Fjords Maritime Museum** (Sudurtangi; open daily May–Sept

Hnífsdalur, on the coast north of Ísafjörður

1–5pm, July 10am–5pm; admission charge). It's in a well-restored timber warehouse and has some fascinating old photographs from the early 20th century. The town has a swimming pool and cinema and a few restaurants and hotels.

About 12km (7 miles) north, **Bolungarvík** is an exposed spot, liable to landslides and avalanches. It has

Arctic fox

a couple of little museums. The **Ósvör Maritime Museum** (open June–mid-Sept Mon–Sat 10am–5pm; admission charge) is in a restored fishing station and the **Natural History Museum** (Aðalstræti 21; open June–Sept Mon–Fri 9am–noon 1–5pm, Sat, Sun 1–5pm; admission charge) has a jumble of stuffed animals including a seal and polar bear. Further west, the coast is largely uninhabited; the scenery is wild and imposing, a mixture of wind-lashed headlands and mighty snow-capped peaks.

Southeast of Ísafjörður, the road winds around several fjords to **Reykjanes**, which is worth a stop for its heated outdoor pool and sauna. If you want to get close to a glacier, continue towards the **Kaldalón glacial lagoon**. From the head of the lagoon you can follow a walking trail for about an hour and a half to the tip of the glacier.

The area further north towards the **Hornstrandir Peninsula** is now uninhabited, after the last family left it in 1995. The beauty of this part of the country, with its sandy bays, rugged cliffs, wild flowers and massive bird colonies, is astonishing. For serious hiking it's hard to beat, and you can literally walk all day without meeting anyone. If you're

Cascading Dynjandi falls

lucky you might spot an Arctic fox and, offshore, whales and seals.

West of Ísafjörður, the road runs through some tiny fishing villages as it heads south. There is a breathtaking descent into **Hrafnseyri**, the birthplace of the Independence leader, Jón Sigurðsson. A small museum is dedicated to his memory (open daily mid-June–Aug 10am–8pm; admission charge), and there is much celebration in the village on Independence Day, 17 June. The **Dynjandi waterfall**, meaning 'the thundering one', just south of here, is spectacular.

Tálknafjörður, to the west, is a lively spot. It has a pool, bike-hire shop, an adventure centre offering watersports and walking, and even a bar. Just outside town there is an open-air geothermal hotpot at **Stóri-Laugardalur**.

At **Látrabjarg**, you are at the most westerly point in Europe. What makes the long journey worthwhile are the amazing **bird cliffs** just outside the village. Thousands of puffins nest here in burrows, and you can get surprisingly close to them. There are at least as many guillemots, too, plus the largest colony of razorbills in the world. Although the noise the birds make can be deafening, the sight is unforgettable.

There is a wonderful **beach** at nearby **Rauðasandur**, with pink sand and superb surf thundering in from the Atlantic. **Hnjótur** is home to a **folk museum** (open daily June–Aug 9am–6pm; admission charge) with an odd-ball collection of marine rescue equipment, old telephones and a typewriter with Icelandic characters. The pride exhibit is a rusting Aeroflot biplane that ended up in Iceland after its pilot, fleeing Russia, was refused permission to land in the US. Outside is a replica Viking longship, a gift from Norway to mark 1,100 years of settlement.

THE WEST COAST

The stretch of coastline south from the West Fjords to Reykjavík is often passed through quickly by visitors on their way to other parts. However, two things in particular bring visitors to the peninsula: the extinct volcano, **Snæfellsjökull**, and **whale-watching** tours from Ólafsvík.

The Snæfellsnes Peninsula

At 1,445m (4,740ft) high **Snæfellsjökull** is permanently snow-capped. It was made famous worldwide by Jules Verne

Fishing fleet at Stykkishólmur harbour

Stykkishólmur, renowned for scallops and halibut

as the entry point for his *Journey to the Centre of the Earth* and also plays a role in *Under the Glacier*, by Nobel Prize-winning Icelandic novelist Halldór Laxness. The glacier is popular for snowmobile tours. The main peak itself is a less daunting climb than it looks, but only experienced climbers should try it, as the weather is always a danger here.

Whale-watching tours (daily June–Aug; book with Eyja-ferdir, tel: 438 1450, or the tourist office, tel: 436 1543) leave **Ólafsvík** by catamaran. This is the best place to spot killer whales, humpbacks and, if you're lucky, the massive blue whale.

Further north, **Stykkishólmur** is an attractive place with brightly painted wooden houses down by the harbour. The town is famous for its scallops and halibut. At the quayside it's possible to take a two-hour birdwatching and scallop-tasting tour. There is an unusual modern **church** overlooking the town with a roof brightly illuminated with thousands of tiny bulbs. Classical music concerts take place on Sundays in summer (admission charge). South of the town, the mountain of **Helgafell**, much talked about in Icelandic folklore, is not much more than a hillock. But it is said you can have three wishes granted if you climb it from the west in silence and then descend to the east without looking back.

Stykkishólmur is the best place to get a ferry out to the delightful island of **Flatey**. It's a sleepy, peaceful little place, with restored wooden houses set among bright yellow fields of buttercups. The eastern part of the island is a **nature reserve** teeming with birdlife. Watch out for the Arctic tern, which seem particularly aggressive here – even the island's sheep aren't immune from their dive-bombing attacks. There is a fine little church, which was painted by the Catalan artist Baltasar in return for free accommodation, and, next door, the oldest and smallest library in Iceland. You can stay overnight in summer, but in winter the island is virtually deserted.

Reykholt and Vicinity

Both its setting and its cultural history make **Reykholt** a place worth visiting. The wide open spaces of its valley setting are refreshing after so many mountains, and this also was the home of Snorri Sturluson, born in 1179 and immortalised by his saga-writing. He was a distinguished scholar but was murdered here in 1241 after falling foul of the Norwegian king. You can visit **Snorralaug**, the bathing pool where he would receive visitors and, beside it, the

Beacon on cliffs

Tumbling falls of Hraunfossar

remains of a tunnel that led to his home. There a fine museum about Sturluson in the **Heimskringla Exhibition Hall** (open daily June– Aug 10am– 6pm; admission charge), next to the church.

At **Húsafell**, to the east, many Icelanders have holiday cottages. There is access from here to a forest and two **glaciers**, Okjökull and Eiríksjökull, as well as a long **lava cave** at Hallmundarhraun. Nearby is the magnificent **Hraunfossar**, a multitude of tiny cascades that tumble into the Hvíta River along a 1-km (½-mile) stretch.

Further north is the farm of **Eiríksstaðir** (open daily June–Aug 10am–5pm; admission charge), from which the Vikings launched their westward voyages of discovery. Erík the Red, after whom the farm is named, went on to discover Greenland, while his son, Leifur, was the first European to set foot in America. There is a reconstruction of the original farm, complete with Viking guides, next to the excavated hall; the latter dates from 890–980.

Borgarnes

Borgarnes, on the windswept west coast route south to Reykjavík, is essentially a service centre for the neighbouring dairy farms. The park, known as **Skallagrímsgarður**, commemorates one of Iceland's first settlers, Skallagrímur Kveldúlfsson, whose burial mound is still visible. His son, Egill, was the hero of *Egill's Saga,* and there is a monument to him by the mound. He was a bit of a thug, but the drowning of his son (also buried here) turned him into a renowned poet.

A short distance north is **Borg á Myrum**, nothing more than a large rock beside a church, where Skallagrímur and his family lived. There is a **statue** by Ásmundur Sveinsson commemorating the poem Egill wrote about the death of his son. The writer Snorri Sturluson, who is thought to have written *Egill's Saga (see page 81),* also lived here.

Akranes

Located just north of Reykjavik, **Akranes** is dominated by fish-processing, trawler production and cement making. More appealing is the **Safnasvæðið á Akranesi** (Akranes Museum Centre; open daily, mid-May–mid-Sept 10am–6pm, mid-Sept–mid-May: 1–6pm; admission charge), east of town. It houses a folk museum with exhibits from land and sea, including trawler-wire cutters from the Cod War with Britain in the 1970s and a well-preserved ketch, one of the first decked fishing boats in Iceland. There is also an exhibition marking Iceland's sporting achievements and the country's largest collection of rocks, minerals and fossils. There are swimming pools and four hotpots adjacent on Garðabraut.

Sturdy Icelandic horses

Jets of steam and hot-water pools at Hveravellir

THE INTERIOR

Iceland's barren interior – a place so desolate that the Apollo astronauts came here to train for their moon landing – can be crossed by two main north–south routes: the Kjölur (F35, also known as the Kjalvegur) and Sprengisandur (F26), both of which are open only once the snow has melted in summer; some of the more minor routes remain closed throughout the summer if conditions are poor. The weather is generally very unpredictable here, so always go prepared for the worst, with plenty of provisions and warm, protective clothing.

Camping is the only form of accommodation, apart from a few huts operated by Ferðafélag Íslands (Touring Club of Iceland, tel: 568 2533). Visitors without transport can take advantage of the scheduled buses that run between Reykjavík and Akureyri via the Kjölur route (daily in July and August) and between Reykjavík and Lake Mývatn via Sprengisandur (twice weekly from mid-July to late August).

The Kjölur Route

Comparatively straightforward to drive, the Kjölur is the most popular crossing through the central highlands. This is the only route through the interior that travellers could consider making in a normal car, although it is still very strongly advisable to travel by four-wheel drive.

Based on an ancient byway used in saga times, it runs from Gullfoss to the Blöndudalur Valley, passing between the Langjökull and Hofsjökull ice-caps. Behind Gullfoss, the River Hvítá flows out of Hvítárvatn, a glacial lake at the foot of Langjökull. From the main route you should be able to see the lake and its glacial spurs, which extend up to its shores.

The route soon reaches its highest point (just over 670m/ 2,200ft), where a memorial stone commemorates the achievements of Geir Zoëga, an engineer who was for many years in charge of building Iceland's roads.

At the centre of the Kjölur plateau, is **Hveravellir**, an extraordinary area of intense geothermal activity, with hot springs, a hot pool where you can bathe, camping facilities and good overnight huts. Also at Hveravellir is a modest stone shelter where the bandit Fjalla Eyvindur and his wife Halla spent a whole winter in hiding in the 18th century.

The northern section of the route, which is less attractive, follows a new track through the reservoir basin created for Blönduvirkjun hydroelectric power station. After crossing the Blanda River at about halfway between Blönduós and Varmahlíð, you will reach the Blöndudalur Valley and then the ring road.

Cauldron on Kjölur plateau

The Sprengisandur Route

The second main crossing through the interior, the Sprengi-sandur route, runs from the Bárðardalur Valley between Akureyri and Lake Mývatn to Þjórsá, east of Selfoss. It is accessible by four-wheel drive only and covers some of the most desolate ground in the country.

There are three main ways to reach the start of the route proper, all of which converge at or near Laugafell at the edge of the Sprengisandur. The most easterly way heads through the Bárðardalur Valley via two waterfalls: Goðafoss and the basalt Aldeyjarfoss. A more central route goes from the end of the Eyjafjörður Valley, past the former farm/weather station at Nyibær, towards Laugafell. The third, most westerly, route meanders through the Vesturdalur Valley, from Skagafjörður, towards the wet grasslands of Orravatnsrústir and Austari Jökulsá, a huge glacial river fed by the Hofsjökull glacier.

At Laugafell, on a ridge leading northwest from the mountain of the same name, there are several warm springs, a warm bathing pool and a tourist hut. Nearby, the gravel expanse of the Sprengisandur begins with magnificent vistas east to Vatnajökull and the smaller Tungnafellsjökull and west to Hofsjökull. A number of river crossings later, the blue tongues of glaciers come into view. A track forking to the east leads off the gravel plain to Gæsavötn, a small yellow-green oasis and crystal-clear lake amid the dark dramatic landscape. Beyond lie the Gæsavatnaleið and Askja routes.

At Nyidalur, close to the geographical centre of Ice-

Bathing in natural hot springs

The rhyolitic hills of the interior

land is a small campsite, on the only patch of green in the area, and several huts. The next stop on the route is shortly after the mountain of Kistualda (790m/2,600 ft). The dusty track south to **Þórisvatn**, Iceland's second largest lake, continues the landscape of glaciers and black gravel plains. Just beyond the lake is the tiny settlement of Hrauneyjafoss, where there is a petrol station, coffee-shop and small guesthouse.

Next is **Landmannalaugar**, part of the Fjallabak Nature Reserve and a good base for the many walks in the area (there are camping and hut facilities here). Landmannalaugar's spectacular rhyolitic hills are bright yellow, green and red, dotted with deep blue lakes, creamy brown plains and snow patches on grey mosses. There are hot springs here, and steam rises from every corner of the valley.

From Landmannalaugar, it is possible either to head southwestwards to meet the ring road near the south coast or southeast to Bláfjall and the coast.

WHAT TO DO

OUTDOOR ACTIVITIES

There can be few better places in the world than Iceland for exploring the great outdoors. Hiking, skiing, snow-mobiling and four-wheel-drive expeditions are all popular here. Horse riding, fishing, birdwatching, whale-watching and white-water rafting also bring many visitors to Iceland.

Walking and Hiking

There are hiking trails throughout Iceland to suit every level. The more ambitious routes require some previous experience, a high level of fitness and good equipment. The weather can change unexpectedly and if you can't read a map and a compass properly then don't attempt the hikes that take you away from populated areas. However, even for the inexperienced there are some great walks.

For advice on safety, protecting the environment and routes in national parks, the best source of information is the **Nature Conservation Agency** (Skúlgata 21, 101 Reykjavík, tel: 570 7400, <www.natturuvernd.is>).

The two organisations that provide information as well as offering guided hikes and details of mountain huts for overnight stays are: **Ferðafélag Íslands** (Touring Club of Ice-land, Mörkin 6, 108 Reykjavík, tel: 568 2533, <www.fi.is>) and **Útivist** (Hallaveigarstigur 1, 101 Reykjavík, tel: 561 4330, <www.utivist.is>). Tourist offices can provide maps and local contacts for guides.

By far the best months for hiking are June, July and August, when the weather is relatively warm, and visibility is at its best. Beginners could start with some of the excellent walking tours of Reykjavík, including the **Seltjarnarnes-Heiðmörk Pathway**. Suggested routes, which vary from one

Hiking country

to six hours in duration, are available from tourist offices.

Every part of the country has its trails. Some of the best areas for walking and hiking include:

Þingvellir National Park. Marked trails around historic sites and lakeland. One option is a full-day hike up Mt Armannsfell.

Þórsmörk Trail. Routes from the relatively gentle to the challenging. There is access to glaciers in this area.

Snæfellsnes Peninsula. A rugged and often wet area. Ascent of the glacier for experienced hikers.

Hornstrandir. One of the wildest and most isolated parts of the country, suitable for the experienced only.

Lake Mývatn. Flat and gentle routes amid terrific scenery.

Jökulsárgljúfur National Park. Well-marked trails at all levels taking from a few hours to four days.

Mt Snæfell. Demanding hikes from Egilsstaðir along the lake and up the mountain.

Lónsöræfi Reserve. A dozen or so tracks close to the immense Vatnajökull glacier.

Hikes into the **interior**, where there are few roads and no villages, can be very tough but rewarding. The mighty rivers make many of the routes and tracks unpassable by foot, but the F35 Kjölur track is passable in summer without a vehicle. Always seek advice from one of the touring organisations *(see page 89)* before setting off. Take plenty of food and water and leave details of your intended route.

Mountaineering

The unstable nature of many of the cliffs in Iceland make them unsuitable for rock-climbing. One good exception is the bird cliffs on **Heimaey** on the Westman Islands, where you can try the traditional cliff-climbing known as *sprengur* with the help of ropes provided.

On the main mountains and glaciers the ascents are usually fairly gentle, although crampons, ropes and ice axes might be needed. Be careful, as inviting-looking snow may hide dangerous fissures in the rock and ice.

Contact the **Icelandic Alpine Club** (Íslenskri Alpaklúbburinn, Mörkin 6, 108 Reykjavík, tel: 568 2533) for information before setting out, and, once you are ready to go, advise the club of your departure and return.

Horse Riding

There have been horses in Iceland for as long as there have been people in the country. They are used for farming and riding and can be hired, with or without guides, from farms and activity centres all over Iceland. You can do treks of up to 10 days, with accommodation in tents or huts. If you are bringing your own equipment or clothing it must be disinfected on arrival. There are many companies organising horse riding and treks; one of the best is eco-travel company, Íshestar (Sörlaskeið 26, 220 Hafnarfjörður, tel: 555 7000, <www. ishestar.is>). The magazine *Eiðfaxi International* (<www. eidfaxi.is>) is published for Icelandic horse lovers worldwide.

Birdwatching

The quantity and variety of bird life in Iceland has really to be seen to be believed. You will find birds all over the country, along the coast and in the mountains, but the best locations are:

Látrabjarg in the West Fjords: the largest bird cliff known in the world, including the biggest colony of razorbills anywhere on earth.

Heimaey: the site of Iceland's largest puffin colony.

Lake Mývatn, in the north: there are more species of breeding ducks here than anywhere in Europe.

Dyrhólaey Cliffs and elsewhere along the south coast has the world's largest skua colony.

The **Icelandic Society for the Protection of Birds** can be contacted at PO Box 5069, 125 Reykjavík, <www.birdlife. net/iceland>.

Iceland's Birdlife

Iceland's exposed northern location means that while as many as 350 species of birds come here every year, relatively few breed, although recent warming of the climate has increased this number. Sea-birds make up the majority, with as many as 13 million breeding pairs. The puffin population alone rises to more than 10 million by late summer. There are also large numbers of waders and wildfowl. Many species are strictly protected by law.

The lesser black-backed gull is the first migrant to arrive, in February/March, but the locals regard the arrival of the golden plover in April as the start of spring. The best time to go birdwatching is in early summer. Many breeds pass through during the last two weeks of May on their way north to Greenland. In early June the resident breeding species begin their mating rituals. It's important not to disturb the birds at this time. In the second half of June the chicks start to hatch and by mid-August they are leaving the nest. While a few breeds migrate to Iceland for the winter, there is not much to see and puffins, for example, will have gone in search of warmer climes.

Fishing

Salmon and trout fishing in Iceland has an international reputation. For salmon the season is from around the third week of June until mid-September, and for trout it's April/May until late September/October, depending on the location. Normally trout fishing permits can be obtained quickly and easily from tourist offices and elsewhere. In some places no permit is required. Salmon permits need to be obtained well in advance. Contact the **National Angling Association** (Bolholt 6, 105 Reykjavík, tel: 553 1510, <www.angling.is>).

Iceland sits in the North Atlantic's best fishing grounds. Sea angling has traditionally been considered an industry rather than a pastime, but it is now also becoming popular as a sport. The season begins in late May and runs until the end of August. Contact **Angling Club Lax-á** (Vatnsendablettur 181, 203 Kópavogur, tel: 557 6100, <www.lax-a.is>).

Snow Sports

Cross-country skiing has been a way of life in many parts of Iceland in the winter, although it's now starting to be developed as a tourist pursuit. **Downhill skiing** and **snowboarding** are increasingly popular. Bláfjöll, just outside Reykjavík, has five ski areas at different levels. In winter, however, the limited daylight makes skiing difficult, although night skiing excursions are available. Kerlingarfjöll, near the Hofsjökull glacier in the interior, has skiing all year round with a summer ski school, but book well in advance.

Skiing is possible all year round

There is good skiing at Akureyri, where the lifts range from 500–1,000m (1,640ft–3,280ft), with more basic runs at Ísafjörður, Eskifjörður, and Siglufjörður. The best time of year for this sport is around March and April. Many tour operators run skiing trips, or check with the Icelandic Alpine Club *(see page 91)*.

Glacier tours with **snowmobiles** are a safe and fun way to see the ice close up. The best take you on to the Vatnajökull glacier in the southeast and the Snæfellsjökull glacier in the west. Contact Icelandic Adventure (Tangarhöfði 7, 112 Reykjavík, tel: 577 5500, <www.adventure.is>) and Allra-handa Excursions (Hyrjarhöfði 2, 110 Reykjavík, tel: 540 1313, <www.allrahanda.is>).

Dog-sledding is a great way to see Iceland's mountains and glaciers. Dog Steam Tours (tel: 487 7747, <www.dogsledding.is>) offers different excursions, on snow or glaciers depending on conditions.

White-Water Rafting

This is a relatively new sport in Iceland but it is growing in popularity. The water can be very cold, but you will be provided with all the right protective gear. There is a minimum age, depending on the risk level. Among the companies organising trips are Activity Tours, based in the north near Sauðárkrókur (PO Box 75, 560 Varmahlíð, tel: 453 8383, <www.rafting.is>) and Icelandic Adventure (Tangarhöfði 7, 112 Reykjavík, tel: 577 5500, <www.adventure.is>).

Speeding on the Skálafellsjökull

Experiencing the thrill of white-water rafting

Swimming

More than just a sport in Iceland, swimming is a social activity for all the family, and there are geothermally heated pools in most towns and many villages. If you want to do serious lengths, the best pool in Reykjavík is at Laugardalur on Sundlaugavegur (tel: 553 4039; open Mon–Fri 5.50am– 9.30pm, Sat, Sun 8am–8pm; admission fee). It has a 50-m (160-ft) pool, four hot pots, a Jacuzzi, steam room, sun lamps and waterslide. Swimming costumes can be hired for a small fee.

Whale-Watching

Whale-watching started in Iceland as recently as 1995, but since then the number of companies offering tours has been increasing all the time. There's a good chance of seeing at least something – most likely the common minke whale, although humpbacks, fin and even blue whales are spotted from time to time, as well as dolphins and porpoises. If you

Rough terrain for cycling

don't see anything at all, most companies will offer you a free second trip.

There are departures from Reykjavík, Hafnarfjörður, Keflavík, Stykkishólmur, Ólafsvík, Heimaey, Dalvík, and Húsavík, where there is a Whale Museum. You don't have to be on a boat to see whales – a glance out to sea might reveal a whale's back breaking the surface.

Cycling

Tim Moore's amusing *Frost on My Moustache* describes a journey across the interior of Iceland by bike, but such a journey should not be taken lightly. Indeed the unmade roads and high winds in much of Iceland can make cycle touring a challenge, to say the least. Off-road cycling is prohibited to help protect the environment.

The **Icelandic Mountain Bike Club** (Íslenska Fjallhjóla-klúbburinn, PO Box 5193, 125 Reykjavík, tel: 562 0099, <www.mmedia.is/~ifhk>) is a great source of advice. In summer months it organises a number of trips around the country that you may be able to join.

Golf

There are more than 25 courses in Iceland, five of which are 18-hole. All the major courses are open to visitors, and fees are very reasonable. For details, contact the **Icelandic Golf Club** (Golfsamband Íslands, Engjavegur 6, 104 Reykjavík, tel: 568 6686). The golf course in Akureyri holds the Arctic Open under the midnight sun every June.

SHOPPING

Iceland isn't a shoppers' paradise, although it does have some interesting local outlets, and a tax-free shopping scheme helps to mitigate the otherwise high prices *(see box below).*

Reykjavik has a good selection of trendy fashion shops for both sexes that are worth a visit, especially when the sales are on. The best shopping street in the capital is Laugavegur, which has a mixture of international names and smaller local retailers. There is an excellent bookshop at No. 18, Mál & Menning, with almost an entire floor given over to titles in English.

The two main shopping centres are Kringlan, on the road of the same name, and Smáralind on Hagasmára in Kópavogur, just outside Reykjavík. Both contain many well-known names as well as cafés and restaurants.

For **souvenirs** try Icelandic woollen sweaters, gloves, scarves and hats. Most are produced by small workshops and come in all shapes, sizes and colours. The Handknitting Association of Iceland's shop at Skólavörðustigur 19 has a wide selection. The same street has a number of **art** galleries selling some excellent local work, as well as **craft shops** for handicrafts, stones and other minerals. Duvets, quilts and

Tax-Free Shopping

It's worth remembering that on departure from Iceland you can get a refund of the VAT (Value Added Tax) paid on goods over 4,000 Ikr provided they were purchased in the previous three months. Ask the shop assistant where you see the 'Tax-Free Shopping' sign, and you will be given a coupon to present at the airport before you leave. If the total is more than 40,000 Ikr, you will have to show the goods themselves on your way out of the country, otherwise just the receipts will do. This scheme can save you about 15 percent on the price of many items.

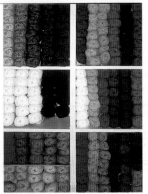

Wool for hand-knitting

other bedcovers are also very good quality, although those filled with locally gathered eider down can be expensive.

Smoked salmon, roe caviar and *skyr*, a delicious Icelandic yoghurt, are good buys, but be aware of the import restrictions on food in your own country.

Icelandic skin- and health-care products are making a name for themselves at home and abroad. The most sought-after are those made at the Blue Lagoon *(see page 37)*, which can be bought in many stores across Iceland, includingthe airport shops.

NIGHTLIFE

In the 1990s Reykjavík developed an almost legendary reputation for its fashionable bars and clubs, but it was always somewhat overstated. It is possible to have an extremely good night out on the town, but that town is still a small one and rather tame compared with many capital cities.

There are dozens of very welcoming bars and cafés for a drink or light meal during the evening, but the serious clubbing doesn't start until well after midnight. Icelanders tend to dress up a bit to go out, and there can be long queues outside the most fashionable places on Friday and Saturday. There is usually an admission charge of at least 1,000 Ikr, and drinks inside don't come cheap.

As with most cities, clubs and pubs open and close in Reykjavík all the time, so it's worth asking around to find out where the newest and most fashionable places are. Publications such as *Netið Info Information for Tourists* and *What's On in Reykjavík* are good starting points. Some of the best clubs that have been around for some time include Café Victor (Hafnarstræti 1–3), Kaffi Reykjavík (Vesturgata 2), Astro (Austurstræti 22) and Spotlight (Hafnarstræti 12).

For more **cultural** nights out, Reykjavík has its own ballet, opera, symphony orchestra and several theatre and dance groups. *What's On in Reykjavík* and local papers list the latest shows. Jazz venues include Kafflelkhúsið (Café Theatre, Vesturgata 3) and the restaurant Jazz at Jómfrúin (Lækjargata 4), which has jazz recitals in summer (Sat 4–6pm).

There are seven cinemas in the capital, and foreign films are shown in their original language with Icelandic subtitles.

Outside the capital nightlife can be hard to find, although Akureyri is becoming increasingly popular. Góði Dátinn

Reykjavík has a good selection of stylish bars

(Geislagata 14, Akureyri) is packed with a young crowd on Friday and Saturday and often has live bands.

ACTIVITIES FOR CHILDREN

Icelanders try to involve children in almost all their sporting and cultural activities. Swimming and horse riding are particularly popular with local children, and families gather in large numbers at weekends to feed the ducks and geese at Tjörn in front of City Hall.

The pool at Laugardalur *(see page 95)* has a huge 85-m (280-ft) waterslide and a children's pool. At the same site, Reykjavík's Family Park and Farmyard Zoo (open daily, summer 10am–6pm, winter Thur–Tues 10am–5pm; admission charge, free for under-fives) is always a hit with the kids, and when they tire of looking at the seals, foxes, reindeer, horses, cows, pigs and all the other animals, they can head for the Family Park. There they can try their hand operating little electric cars, pull themselves across a man-made lake on a raft, climb a replica Viking ship and more. There is a large grill that can be used free of charge for barbecuing. The seals are fed twice a day (11am and 4pm).

Off for a ride

For older children there are two bowling rinks, Keiluhöllin at Öskjuhlíð (open Sun–Tues noon–midnight, Fri, Sat noon–2am) and Keila at Mjódd (open Mon–Fri noon–11.30pm, Sat, Sun 10am–11.30pm).

The Volcano Show (Hellusund 6), is a fascinating-film display featuring eruptions, including that of Surtsey island *(see page 30)*.

Calendar of Events

The precise dates of events change from year to year as they are linked to religious holidays or the seasons. Check with tourist offices for details.

January 6 Twelfth Night, marked with songs, bonfires and fireworks.

Late January Þorri. The half-way point of winter, this festival involves eating delicacies including lambs' heads and testicles and cured shark.

Early February Festival of Lights. Reykjavík's winter festival with arts and cultural events.

Ash Wednesday A children's carnival ends three days of events. Cream buns are consumed on 'Bun Day', the Monday, followed by enormous meat dishes on Tuesday, 'Bursting Day'.

End of April The First Day of Summer. Children's events in most towns, with parades, fairs and flag days.

1st Sunday in June Festival of the Sea. Celebrations in all coastal communities with sports and dances.

17 June National Day. Formal ceremonies in the morning and partying and fairs all afternoon and evening.

Late June Akureyri Theatre Festival. Street artists, puppet shows and major productions.

Early July Landsmót National Horse Show, Skagafjörður.

Late July Week-long Whale Festival, Húsavík.

1st Monday in August Summer Bank Holiday. A long weekend for all Icelanders, with open-air pop festivals around the country.

3rd Saturday in August Reykjavík's birthday celebrations with cultural events of all kinds. The City Marathon is held on the same day.

September/October Reykjavík Film Festival featuring both Icelandic and international movies.

Late October Iceland Airwaves. A four-day contemporary music event with top-class bands from all over the world.

23rd December St Þorláksmessa. Traditional feasts mark one of Iceland's few indigenous saints and the high point of the pre-Christmas celebrations.

31st December New Year's Eve. A satirical revue on television, followed by outdoor parties that can last all night.

EATING OUT

Going for a meal in Iceland is a highly variable business – usually, the only thing you can be sure of is that you will feel you have paid a huge amount for what you have just eaten. Although the situation is improving year by year, in some parts of the country it can be hard to find anything much more than a very basic meal of meat or fish plus vegetables. There may be a pizzeria in town if you're lucky, but in some small towns there is just a grill bar at the fuel station.

At the other end of the scale, in Reykjavík and the more expensive hotels around the country, you can eat very well – but at a high price.

Iceland was effectively cut off from the rest of Europe for centuries, and, with very little in the way of food imports, no Icelandic *haute cuisine* developed. The population depended on what they could catch or grow themselves, making do with a diet based almost entirely on fish, lamb and vegetables such as potatoes. Various methods were devised to

Meal Times

Icelanders tend to have their main meal in the middle of the day and this is also when you can find some of the better priced all-inclusive menus (often restricted to around noon–2.30pm). In Reykjavík and many of the larger towns, restaurants tend to be open all day from about 11.30am until 11pm (later at weekends), so you don't have to be too organised about when you eat. In some smaller places, cafés and restaurants shut at about 2.30pm and reopen around 7pm. They close anytime after 10pm, so it's always a good idea to check their opening times before planning your evening. Breakfast hours are relaxed, so you don't usually have to be up too early to fit in with them.

Haddock and cod being dried to store for winter

preserve the food so it could be used for months after it was caught. Meat was smoked, salted and pickled. Fish would be hung out and dried, or smoked in dung or salted, or even buried. You will still occasionally see fish-drying racks on the hillsides as you drive around the country.

Traditional Foods

The two staple foods are fish and lamb. Fish is most plentiful and cheaper, so every meal, from breakfast onwards, will usually include it in some form.

The fish you see drying in the wind on racks is haddock or cod used to make *harðfiskur*. It's torn into strips and eaten as a snack, sometimes with butter, with a glass of milk or maybe something stronger.

If you are feeling brave, and think your stomach can take it, search out some *hákarl* – putrified shark meat. It's buried, usually in sand and gravel, for up to six months, which

> **Ice-covered land and frozen seas forced Icelanders to preserve their fish and meat, so it could be stored and eaten all winter long.**

breaks down the ammonia and toxins in the flesh – there is no mistaking the stench of ammonia when it's dug up again. The shark meat is washed down with a strong liquor known as *brennivín*, which helps to take away some of the taste. The darker meat on the shark, *gler hákarl*, is a little less potent than the white meat, but either way it's an eye-watering experience, to put it very mildly. Occasionally you will find on the menu whale meat that has been stored in the same way; however, as hunting whales for food has been forbidden since 1989, the meat is either from a whale that beached and died or was illegally caught.

Most Icelandic seafood, by contrast, is absolutely delicious and comes to your plate very fresh indeed. Icelandic cod, halibut, turbot and monkfish, for example, are juicy and succulent. Salmon and trout from the rivers are large and relatively inexpensive, as is char, a species of trout that is found all over Iceland. Smoked salmon and gravadlax (smoked salmon marinated with herbs) are both of very high quality.

While you will never go short of tasty fish, you might tire of it after a while. The other Icelandic staple, lamb, may cost more, but the taste is exceptional. Sheep farms on the island are small, and the flocks are allowed to graze wild in the highlands, where they eat herbs as well as grass. As a result, the meat has quite a gamey flavour.

As with fish, lamb was traditionally smoked to produce *hangikjöt,* which is eaten hot or cold. Nothing was ever allowed to go to waste in winter in Iceland, and dishes made of sheep's offal are still produced. *Slátur* (literally: slaughter) is a haggis-like dish made from all manner of left-overs, pressed into cakes, pickled in whey and cooked in stomach lining. Alternatively *svið* are boiled and singed sheep's heads, minus the brains, that are eaten either fresh or pickled. The meat is sometimes then taken off the bone and pressed to produce *sviðasulta*. A real delicacy, served on special occasions, is *súrsaðir hrútspungar* (pickled rams' testicles).

A limited amount of game finds its way on to the dinner plate. Reindeer from the east of the country is similar to venison. Ptarmigan is a grouse-like bird and a favourite at Christmas time. Icelanders are quite happy to eat their national symbol, too: puffin is often seen on the menu; it is frequently smoked and produces quite a dark, rich meat.

The main locally produced vegetables are potatoes and turnips. Wild berries are often used in sauces and puddings, and rhubarb thrives in the cold climate. Otherwise the dessert course is often cakes or pastries. One delicious treat is *skyr,* a yoghurt-type dish made of pasteurised skimmed milk and live

Sushi chef, Reykjavík

> **Drinking beer was illegal in Iceland from 1912–89. Its reintroduction – on 1 March 1989 – is celebrated annually as *Bjórdagurinn* (beer day).**

bacteria; it's often mixed with fruit flavouring and is very low in fat.

Bread, often made with rye, is a normal accompaniment to any meal. It may be baked in underground ovens in the naturally hot earth to produce *hverabrauð* ('steam bread'). Rye pancakes, known as *flatkaka*, go well with smoked salmon and other *smorgasbord*-type toppings.

What to Drink

Not surprisingly, the Icelandic climate is not conducive to wine-growing, so all wines are imported and ruinously expensive. There are high taxes on all alcohol, since – in common with other Nordic countries – the government tries to discourage alcoholism. It's not that long ago that beer was actually illegal on the island *(see box above)*.

Even today alcohol can only be bought from bars, restaurants and licensed government liquor stores known as *áfengisbúðar* (ÁTVR). They have strictly limited opening times (Mon–Thur 11am–6pm, Fri 11am–7pm, Sat 11am–2pm). The only exception is the very weak beer known as *pilsner,* which is less than 2.2 percent proof and inexpensive.

Icelandic spirits, on the other hand, are both strong and tasty. *Brennivín* ('burnt wine') is a schnapps distilled from potatoes and flavoured with caraway seeds. Its nickname is 'Black Death', but don't let that put you off. A good variant is *Hvannarótar*, which is flavoured with angelica.

When they are not drinking alcohol, Icelanders are very keen on coffee, and there are coffee shops everywhere. It's sometimes even offered free from flasks in libraries, shops and supermarkets. Tea is less common than coffee, but is widely available.

If the Menu isn't in English....

Gætum við/get ég fengið…Could we/I have…

Basics

ávextir	fruit
bakað	baked
baunir	peas, beans
kartöflur	potatoes
brauð	bread
glóðað	grilled
grænmeti	vegetables
hrísgrjón	rice
kartöflur	potatoes
laukur	onion
ostar	cheeses
reykt	smoked
salat	salad
smjör	butter
súpa	soup
smárettir	snacks
soðið	boiled
steikt	fried

Drinks

appelsínusafi	orange juice
bjór	beer
kaffi	coffee
mjólk	milk
te	tea
vatn	water
vín	wine
(hrauðvín)	(red)
(hvítvín)	(white)

Fiskur (Fish)

bleikja	char
hörpuskel	scallop
humar	lobster
lax	salmon
lúða	halibut
rauðspretta	plaice
sandhverfa	turbot
síld	herring
siltungur	trout
skötuselur	monkfish
steinbítur	catfish
Ysa	haddock
rækja	shrimp
Þorskur	cod

Kjöt (Meat)

lambakjöt	lamb
lundi	puffin
nautakjöt	beef
lambakótelettur	lamb chop
nautalundir	beef fillet
nautasteik	beef steak
skinka	ham
kjúklingur	chicken
svínakjöt	pork
lítið steikt	rare
miðlungs steikt	medium
vel steikt	well done

HANDY TRAVEL TIPS

An A–Z Summary of Practical Information

A

ACCOMMODATION (See also CAMPING, YOUTH HOSTELS, and the list of RECOMMENDED HOTELS on page 130)

The Icelandic Tourist Board has recently introduced a classification system for accommodation, but not all hotels have signed up to it. The system grades hotels from four stars, for those with the best facilities, down to one star, for the most basic.

Both in Reykjavík and elsewhere in the country many of the higher-rated hotels are large and impersonal. The capital has some quality hotels with character, and there are one or two elsewhere in the country, but these are the exception. The smaller, family-run Icelandic hotels can be quite spartan. In some towns schools and colleges are converted into hotels for the summer months and can be good value. If you are doing a lot of walking or horse riding check if the hotel has a sauna, hot-tub or pool, all of which will be geothermally heated.

There are guesthouses everywhere in Iceland and these are generally welcoming and considerably cheaper than hotels. They vary in quality, but are invariably clean and well-kept. Bathrooms are very often shared. Farmhouse accommodation is also available. More than 130 farms operate through Icelandic Farm Holidays (tel: 570 2700, <www.farmholidays.is>).

If you are travelling around, the location of a hotel will probably be more important to you than its facilities. Local tourist offices *(see page 128)* have comprehensive lists of nearby hotels and staff who can speak English and make reservations for you. If you are travelling between May and September you are advised to book ahead.

AIRPORTS

Iceland's **Keflavík** international airport (tel: 425 0680), 55km (35 miles) west of Reykjavík, is huge, and the signposting there isn't that easy to follow. There are Foreign Exchanges both before and after passport control. There are also ATMs, which accept most cards. Duty-free wine and spirits on arrival are much cheaper than in hotels and restaurants. Car-rental offices are in the arrivals hall.

The airport bus costs 1000 Ikr and takes 45 minutes. It goes first to the Loftleiðir hotel, with transfers on to the domestic airport and some of the bigger hotels.

Taxis from the airport to central Reykjavík will take about half an hour and cost upwards of 7,200 Ikr.

Reykjavík's domestic airport is at the other end of the runway from the Loftleiðir hotel. There are regular buses to and from the city centre on route No. 5.

B

BICYCLE HIRE

Tourist offices and hotels will have details of bike rental. The long-distance bus company, BSÍ (tel: 562 3320, <www.bsi.is>), hires good-quality mountain bikes and accessories, with discounts available if you have one of its bus passes.

BUDGETING FOR YOUR TRIP

Iceland is undoubtedly an expensive location, but with careful planning the costs can be brought down significantly.

Getting to Iceland. Icelandair's long-standing monopoly traditionally meant very high airfares. In Spring 2003 a new budget airline IcelandExpress (tel: 550 0650, <www.icelandexpress.com>) started operations with fares from just £108 return from London Stansted. The cheapest-published fares with Icelandair (tel: 505 0700) start at £310 from London Heathrow to Reykjavík and £250 from Glasgow to Reykjavík. There are sometimes cheaper so-called Lucky Fares (upwards of £130) on the Icelandair website <www.icelandair.co.uk>, although availability is limited. If you are flying from the US, Icelandair is still the only option, and you can expect to pay from $700 for a return ticket. Check on <www.icelandair.net> for offers.

Travelling to Iceland by Smyril Line ferry (<www.smyril-line.fo>) is expensive. A return ticket with a bed in a cabin in high season from the Shetland Islands to Seyðisfjörður is upwards of £272.

Accommodation. The more-expensive hotels can charge over 20,000 Ikr a night for a double room in high season, but you can get a good-standard hotel in the region of 12,000 Ikr in Reykjavík and 9,000 Ikr elsewhere. Guesthouses charge around 6–7,000 Ikr. In some places you can pay about half the price if you use your own sleeping-bag.

Meals. Dining out costs anything up to 10,000 Ikr a head, without wine, in the best Reykjavík restaurants; wine is extremely expensive across the entire country, and you will be lucky to find a decent bottle for less than 2,000 Ikr. Dinner in a mid-range hotel might cost 4–5,000 Ikr, again without wine. Check the prices in restaurant windows – you should be able to find a reasonable meal for less than 2,000 Ikr. Lunchtime specials tend to be good value.

Local transport. A Reykjavík bus ticket costs 200 Ikr, but long-distance journeys are expensive by comparison. A bus from the Reykjavík to Akureyri, for example, is 5,300 Ikr one-way, to Egilsstaðir 10,620 Ikr. There are various passes available from the bus company BSÍ (tel: 562 3320, <www.bsi.is>) and these will entitle you to discounts on ferries and at some campsites, too.

Domestic flights are generally cheaper than buses. The same journey from the capital to Akureyri costs from 4,400 Ikr single, and to Egilsstaðir 5,200kr. Air Iceland also has an air-pass for between four and six flights, but these must be bought outside the country. Taxis cost about 1,000 Ikr for a short journey in town.

Incidentals. Bus and coach tours are good value. A sightseeing tour of Reykjavík costs 2,100 Ikr per person, and a half-day tour to the nearest falls and geysers is 4–5,000 Ikr. Whale-watching costs between 3,000 and 4,500 Ikr. Car hire costs a minimum of 4,500 Ikr per day, with limited mileage, and a full tank of petrol costs around 5,000 Ikr. Entrance to nightclubs is at least 1,000 Ikr; once inside, beers cost 500 Ikr or more each. A coffee is 150 Ikr – more in fashionable drinking holes. A cinema ticket costs 700 Ikr.

C

CAMPING

There are about 125 official campsites in Iceland, although you can camp almost anywhere if you get the landowners' permission. Within national parks and conservation areas, camping is only allowed at designated spots.

Official campsites are found in most towns and villages, at national parks, conservation areas, places of natural beauty and some farms and community centres. The standard varies. Expect to pay 350–650 Ikr per person per night for a layer of pumice and an earth closet to soft turf and hot showers. The recognised sites are open from June to August or mid-September.

A leaflet listing campsites is published by the Iceland Tourist Board *(see page 128)*. Equipment can be hired from Sportleigan, Laugavegur 25, Reykjavík, tel: 551 9800, fax: 561 3082.

CAR HIRE (See also DRIVING and BUDGETING FOR YOUR TRIP)

Several major international rental companies are represented in Iceland, as well as locally based firms. Prices are high. You must be at least 20 years old to hire a car in Iceland. Insurance is compulsory and not always included in the quoted price, so check first.

The bigger companies are Hertz (tel: 505 0600), Europcar (tel: 568 6915), Avis (tel: 533 1090) and Budget (tel: 567 8300). Local companies include ALP (tel: 567 0722) and Bílaleiga Íslands (tel: 588 6808).

Unmade roads, especially in the interior, require a substantial car, usually a four-wheel drive. Note that insurance does not usually cover you to travel in the interior – check this very carefully before hiring a vehicle.

CLIMATE

Despite its name, Iceland isn't *that* cold. It benefits from the gulf stream and is warmer than much of Scandinavia, for example. However, summers are generally cool, and the country is often wet and windy, with the weather changing dramatically from day to day as well as within one day itself. Basically, it's sensible to be prepared for all eventualities. The weather is drier and sunnier in the north and east than the south and west, although no less windy. The south coast is notoriously wet.

You can get weather information in English by calling 902 0600 ext. 44 or visiting <www.vedur.is/english>.

Average rainfall and temperatures:

	J	F	M	A	M	J	J	A	S	O	N	D
°C min	-2	-2	-1	1	4	7	9	8	6	3	0	-2
°C max	2	3	4	6	10	12	14	14	11	7	4	2
Rainfall mm	76	72	82	58	44	50	52	62	66	85	72	79

CLOTHING

Although in summer you may be warm enough in a T-shirt and shorts, it's sensible to pack for bad weather all year round, with the more layers the better. Waterproof clothing is essential, and if you are planning to spend a lot of time outdoors invest in windproof outer garments. Take plenty of jumpers to keep you warm plus thick walking socks (and thinner ones to go against your skin).

Icelanders don't dress up to go out, unless they are going to very expensive restaurants – even there, you wouldn't be expected to wear a tie. The younger clubbing crowd is very fashion conscious, but you won't be turned away from a venue for wearing jeans or trainers.

Pack a swimming costume, as heated outdoor pools are very much a part of the Icelandic social scene.

CRIME AND SAFETY (See also EMERGENCIES and POLICE)

Iceland is an extremely peaceful and law-abiding nation. Of the few people in prison most are drugs offenders. Public places are well lit. Pickpocketing and street crime are rare, although Reykjavík has a number of drug addicts and alcoholics who steal to fund their habits, so some caution is always sensible. Drunken crowds of young people in the streets of Reykjavík in the early hours at week-ends can be intimidating, but rarely threatening.

CUSTOMS AND ENTRY REQUIREMENTS

Iceland has signed the Schengen Agreement, so, in principle, residents of other Schengen countries (Norway plus all EU countries except Britain and Ireland) can travel without document checks. Flights from the UK go through passport control. Iceland doesn't require visas from citizens of EU states, the US, Canada, Australia or New Zealand; South African citizens do require one. Passports must be valid for at least three months after your arrival date, and visitors may stay for that period. There are no currency restrictions.

D

DRIVING

Despite the high cost of car hire, rental may provide the only way to see everything you wish in the time available. Driving in Iceland can also be a real pleasure – the roads are not busy and the freedom to stop to admire the scenery or go for a walk is a huge bonus. Be prepared for journeys to take a lot longer than you might expect from the distances involved.

Road conditions. While much of the main highway encircling the country is surfaced, many routes in Iceland are just gravel or unmade and full of potholes. Some roads are prone to flooding, and bridges are often single-lane.

Icelanders drive surprisingly fast, often in the middle of the road, making way for oncoming vehicles at the last minute.

Sandstorms can be a hazard along the coast and in some parts of the interior. In winter, snow and ice are common, and studded snow tyres are essential.

For information on road conditions tel: 1777 between 8am and 4pm or check on <www.vegag.is>.

Rules and regulations. Icelanders drive on the right. The speed limit is 50km/h (30mph) in urban areas, 80km/h (50mph) on gravel roads in rural areas and 90km/h (55mph) on asphalt roads out of the towns.

Driving off roads is illegal, seat belts are compulsory in the front and back of a car, and headlights must be used at all times, day and night. Drink-driving, which is defined as 0.05 percent blood-alcohol content, is taken very seriously by the authorities. Offenders lose their licences and face heavy fines.

Fuel. In Reykjavík most filling stations stay open until 11.30pm. Many have automatic pumps that take credit cards after that time. Around the ring road there are filling stations every 50km (30 miles) or so, but if in doubt fill up before you move on. Prices vary, but it will cost about 5,000 Ikr to fill up the tank of a medium-sized saloon car.

Parking. Reykjavík has plenty of parking meters, ticket machines and car parks, some of which are covered and attended. On-street parking can be hard to find. Elsewhere in the country you will encounter few problems, and there are large free car parks at most of the major tourist sites.

Road signs. The usual international symbols are used on road signs, but look out also for:

Einbreið brú	Single-lane bridge (often marked by flashing orange lights)
Malbik endar	Unmade road
Blindhæð	Blind summit

Help and information. Tourist boards have leaflets about driving on unmade roads and in winter, as well as lists of all road signs. You can also contact Félag Íslenskra Bifreiðaegenda (Icelandic Automobile Association; tel: 562 9999).

E

ELECTRICITY

The current in Iceland is 220 volts, 50 HZ AC. Plugs are round pin with two or three prongs.

EMBASSIES/CONSULATES

Australia: Australian citizens must contact the embassy in Copenhagen, Denmark, tel: (+45) 70 26 36 76, fax: (+45) 70 26 36 86, <australian.embassy@mail.dk>.
Canada: Túngata 14, 101 Reykjavík, tel: 575 6500, fax: 575 6501, <embassy.canada@mmedia.is>.
Ireland: Consul General, Mávanes 7, 210 Garðabær, tel: 554 2355.

South Africa: Hús Verslunarinnar, Kringlunni 7, Reykjavík, tel: 520 3300, fax: 520 3399, <jr@sr-mjol.com>.
United Kingdom: Laufásvegur 31, 101 Reykjavík, tel: 550 5100, fax: 550 5105, <www.britishembassy.is>.
United States: Laufásvegur 21, 101 Reykjavík, tel: 562 9100, fax: 562 9529, <www.usa.is>.
The Icelandic Foreign Ministry has a full list of diplomatic representatives on its website: <utanrikisraduneyti.is>.

EMERGENCIES (See also HEALTH and MEDICAL CARE on page 119)

To contact the police, ambulance or fire service, tel: **112**.
For the Emergency Room at Reykjavík City Hospital, tel: 525 1700; outside the capital ask for the nearest Health Centre.
Chemists are signed *Apótek,* and there is at least one in every town. Háaleitis Apótek in the Austurver mini-mall, Háaleitisbraut 68, Reykjavík (tel: 581 2101) is open daily 8am–2am.
In case of dental emergencies, tel: 568 1041.

G

GAY AND LESBIAN TRAVELLERS

For its size, Reykjavík has a large and visible gay and lesbian community, although outside the capital there is virtually no commercial scene.

The Reykjavík Gay Community Centre is in the centre of town on the fourth floor at Laugavegur 3 (open Mon–Fri 2–4pm, Mon, Thur, Sat 8–11pm; tel: 552 7878, <www.gayiceland.com>). It's a friendly place with a coffee bar, and a book and video library, and alcoholic drinks are available in the evenings.

There are no exclusively gay bars in Iceland, but the nightclub Spotlight (Hafnastræti 12, tel: 562 6813, <www.spotlight.is>) is very popular with gays. So, too, is Nelly's Café/Bar (Þingholtsstræti 2, tel: 562 1250). A gay men's leather club runs every

Saturday at Bankastræti 11 (from 11pm; tel: 562 1280, <www.
this.is/msc>). There is an annual Gay Pride celebration in Reykjavík every August, <www.this.is/gaypride>.

GETTING THERE (See also AIRPORTS and BUDGETING)

The fastest and cheapest way to get to Iceland is by air. Icelandair
flies at least once daily from London Heathrow and daily except
Saturday from Glasgow. From London Stansted there is a daily
flight with IcelandExpress. From the United States, Icelandair
operates from five cities: Baltimore, Boston, Minneapolis, Orlando
and New York.

From May to September the Faroese company, Smyril Line
<www.smyril-line.fo>, runs a weekly ferry between Hanstholm
(Denmark), Tórshavn (Faroe Islands), Bergen (Norway) and Lerwick (Shetland Islands) to Seyðsfjörður in eastern Iceland. Ferry
connections for Lerwick are available from Aberdeen. A through
journey from London to Iceland using the ferry takes four days,
departing Monday arriving Thursday.

GUIDES AND TOURS (See also PUBLIC TRANSPORT)

One of the best ways of seeing the main sites is by organised coach
tours. The drivers and tour leaders are always well informed and
speak English. If you want to travel into the interior or on to glaciers, a tour is often the only choice.

Tours are well run, and many allow you to do some exploring by
yourself. Those operated by the bus company BSÍ, tel: 562 3320,
<www.bsi.is>, are little more than regular journeys with stops at the
main points of interest along the way.

Tours can last from half a day to three weeks. As well as sight-
seeing there are tours specialising in hiking, geology, birdwatching,
fishing, glaciers, horse riding and whale-watching.

Sports-orientated tours have good-quality equipment and guides
who are fully trained for the environment.

For the more popular routes, such as the Golden Circle outside Reykjavík and whale-watching, it's worth shopping around, as several operators will be offering much the same service, perhaps at differing prices. Note that many tours do not operate in 'winter' (generally September to May).

For full details, contact the Icelandic Tourist Office *(see page 128)* or look on their website, <www.icetourist.is>, where there is a list of authorised operators and travel agencies.

H

HEALTH AND MEDICAL CARE (See also EMERGENCIES)

Thanks to its clean air and low pollution, Iceland is an extremely healthy place. The water is clean to drink, although you should never drink from glacial rivers or streams. No vaccinations are required to visit Iceland.

Despite the high latitude, the Icelandic sun can still burn, especially when reflected off snow and ice. Sunblock and good sunglasses should be worn if you are outside for long periods. Windburn can cause chafing of the lips and dehydration. Wearing hats and other protection will help, as will a good moisturiser and drinking plenty of fluids.

In extreme circumstances hypothermia is a possibility. It's best avoided by careful planning, wearing layers of warm clothing, taking plenty of rest breaks and eating and drinking sensibly. Symptoms include shivering, numbness, dizzy spells and confused behaviour. If affected, take shelter, remove and replace wet clothing, and consume hot drinks and high-calorie food.

Every year all too mnay visitors are injured, sometimes very seriously, by putting feet or hands into boiling hot mud pools and springs, so take good care to avoid this.

The standard of medical care is very high in Iceland. There is a reciprocal agreement with the UK and Scandinavian countries allowing citizens to receive free health care. However, it doesn't cover prescriptions and some ambulance services. Charges for basic treatment are not particularly high, but good health insurance is recommended nonetheless.

If you are planning to take part in any unusual or 'dangerous' sports, make sure that these are covered by your policy. You may have to pay first and reclaim the costs when you get home, so keep all bills and other documentation.

HOLIDAYS

The following are public holidays in Iceland. Note that most businesses, banks and shops will be closed on these days, and public transport will be more limited than usual.

1 January	New Year's Day
1 May	Labour Day
17 June	National Day
24 December	Christmas Eve (from noon)
25 December	Christmas Day
26 December	Boxing Day
31 December	New Year's Eve (from noon)

Movable dates:
Maundy Thursday
Good Friday
Easter Sunday
Easter Monday
First day of summer
Ascension Day
Whit Sunday
Whit Monday
Bank Holiday Monday (first Monday in August)

L

LANGUAGE

Icelandic is a Germanic language and has barely changed since Viking times. Although it is grammatically complex, anyone who speaks one of the other Scandinavian languages or German will recognise words and features. Thankfully, though, there is no need to master Icelandic to enjoy a holiday in Iceland, since nearly all Icelanders speak excellent English. The Icelandic section of the *Berlitz Scandinavian Phrase Book and Dictionary* covers most situations you are likely to encounter. For some of the most important words and phrases, see below.

Yes	**Já**
No	**Nei**
Hello/hi	**Halló/hæ**
Good morning/afternoon	**Góðan dáginn**
Good evening	**Gott kvöld**
Good night	**Góða nótt**
Goodbye	**Bless**
How do you do?	**Sæll (to a man); sæl (to a woman)**
Fine, thanks	**Mél liður vel, takk**
Thank you	**Takk fyrir**
Yesterday/today/tomorrow	**Í gær/í dag/á morgun**
Where/when/how?	**Hvar/hvenær/hvernig?**
How long/how far	**Hvað lengi/hversu langt**
Left/right	**Vinstri/hægri**
Hot/cold	**Heitt/kalt**
Old/new	**Gamalt/ungt**
Open/closed	**Opið/lokað**
Vacant/occupied	**Laus/upptekinn**
Early/late	**Snemma/seint**

M

MAPS

Good maps are essential to explore Iceland properly, and there are a large number available. Tourist offices have leaflets with basic maps and also sell more detailed ones.

The best maps are those produced by the Icelandic National Land Survey, *Landmælingar Íslands*. This company publishes a 1:500,000 road map of the whole country and also a series of nine 1:250,000 sheets for all regions – these regional maps are detailed enough for hiking.

Less detailed are those produced by *Mál og Menning* in its *Íslandkort* series. These are widely available in shops and at filling stations. *Mál og Menning* also publishes a series of geological maps, *Náttúrufarskort*.

MEDIA

English-language newspapers and magazines are on sale in Reykjavík, usually several days after publication in their home country. They can also be found in public libraries.

Local papers and magazines are almost all in Icelandic, although there is a daily news-sheet, *Icelandic Review* (<www.icenews.is>), which is available at some newsagents and hotels. Two magazines, *Iceland Review* (<www.icelandreview.com>) and *Icelandic Geographic* (<www.icelandgeographic.is>) are published in English; both publications are notable for their informative articles and magnificent photography.

The main national newspaper, *Morgunblaðið,* has daily news in English on its website, <www.mbl.is>.

Many hotels have satellite television, with English and American channels. From 1 June to 1 September, national radio broadcasts the news in English at 7.30am on FM 93.5 and FM 92.4. This programme can also be heard by telephone, on 515 3690.

MONEY (See also BUDGETING FOR YOUR TRIP)

The Icelandic currency is the *króna,* usually abbreviated to Ikr. Banknotes come in 500, 1,000, 2,000 and 5,000 Ikr denominations, and there are 100, 50, 10, 5 and 1 Ikr coins.

Currency Exchange. Foreign exchange is available at all three chains of the Icelandic banks, Íslandsbanki, Landsbanki Ísland and Búnaðarbanki, which charge a nominal commission or sometimes nothing at all. Banks open from 9.15am–4pm and offer the best rates of exchange. Out of banking hours you can exchange money at major hotels or the Change Group, which has branches in Reykjavík and Akureyri and stays open late. Banks and the Change Group can also arrange International Money Transfers.

At the time of going to press, the rate of exchange was as follows: £1 = 127.5 Ikr; €1 = 87.5 Ikr; $1 = 77.35 Ikr.

Credit Cards. Credit cards, in particular Visa and MasterCard, are accepted almost everywhere, although guesthouses may take cash only. Íslandsbanki also accepts Diners Club. Banks and some larger post offices give cash advances against credit cards. American Express customers are advised to call (+44) 1273 571600 to find out where their card will be accepted.

ATMs. There are cash machines at the airport and at many banks. This is often the cheapest way of getting money if your card is part of the international Visa, Cirrus, Maestro and Electron networks. The charges will depend on your bank, but the rate of exchange is generally better than any other method.

Travellers Cheques. These are still accepted, although fewer people than in previous years. To cash travellers cheques, you need also to show your passport.

O

OPENING TIMES

Shops, banks and other services rarely close for lunch. In general their opening hours are:

Banks: 9.15am–4pm

Post Offices: 8.30am–4.30pm

Shops: Mon–Sat 9am–6pm. Smaller shops may not open until 10am. Supermarkets open Sun 10am–2 or 6pm.

Liquor Stores: Mon–Thur 11am–6pm, Fri 11am–7pm, Sat 11am–2pm.

P

POLICE *Lögregla*

In such a law-abiding country the police keep a low profile, and you are unlikely to come across them unless you commit a motoring offence. They can normally speak some English.

Police Emergency Number, tel: **112**.

Reykjavík Police Headquarters is at Hverfisgata 113–115, tel: 569 9020. The Reykjavík city-centre police station is at Tryggvagata 19, tel: 569 9025.

For lost property, contact the police station at Borgartún 33, Reykjavík, tel: 569 9018 (open Mon–Fri 10am–noon and 2pm–4pm).

POST OFFICES

The Icelandic postal service is efficient, and there are post offices (open Mon–Fri 8.30am–4.30pm) in every town. The office at Grensásvegur 9, Reykjavík, is also open on Saturday, 10am–2pm.

It takes up to five days for post to reach Europe or North America and 10 days for Australia, New Zealand and South Africa.

All post offices offer international express mail, TNT and poste restante facilities. If you are receiving mail, ensure that the sender underlines your surname or writes it in capital letters, as Icelanders sort by the first name.

At the time of publication, a letter weighing less than 20g (0.7oz) costs 60 Ikr to Europe and 85 Ikr to the rest of the world. The prices for a letter between 20g and 50g (1.75oz) are 115 Ikr and 160 Ikr. There are up-to-date prices and information at <www.postur.is>.

PUBLIC TRANSPORT

Buses. There is an excellent system of buses both in Reykjavík and across the country. In the capital there are two terminals for the yellow city buses, one near the harbour at Lækjartorg, at the junction of Lækjargata and Austurstræti, and the other at Hlemmur and the far end of the main shopping street, Laugavegur.

Maps showing all the routes are available from terminals and tourist offices.

Services run Mon–Fri, 7am–midnight, and Sun 10am–midnight. There is a flat fare of 200 Ikr, which must be paid in exact change as you board.

If you are changing buses ask for a *skiftimiði*, which is valid on all buses for 45 minutes. A strip of 10 tickets, *eitt kort,* costs 1,500 Ikr. A 30-day Green Card, offering unlimited travel, costs 3,800 Ikr. Children under six years old travel free, and there are reduced fares for under 18 year olds.

Long-distance buses operate from the BSÍ Coach Terminal, Vatnsmõrarvegur (tel: 552 2300, <www.bsi.is>). There are a variety of passes available if you are going to use the bus network extensively. The Full-Circle Passport allows you to travel once round the country in either direction, stopping as often as you like. The Omnibus Passport allows unrestricted travel for between one and four weeks.

Taxis. Taxis are available in all the major towns and cost about 1,000 Ikr for 3km. There are ranks in Reykjavík on Lækjargata and

Eiríksgata. To order a cab by phone call: Borgarbill, tel: 552 2440; BSR, tel: 561 0000; or Hreyfill, tel: 588 5522.

Taxis offer sight-seeing tours at around 3,000 Ikr an hour.

Flights. Air Iceland is the biggest domestic carrier, running flights to the larger towns throughout the country (tel: 570 3030, <www.airiceland.is>). An Air Iceland Pass with four, five or six sectors valid for 30 days, and a Fly As You Please Pass, allowing 12 days unlimited travel on domestic flights, can only be purchased before you enter Iceland.

Íslandsflug is a smaller domestic carrier, operating flights to the Westman Islands and other destinations, mainly in the south and west (tel: 570 8030, <www.islandsflug.is>).

Ferries. Herjólfur runs ferries to the Westman Islands (tel: 481 2800, <www.herjolfur.is>). Seators/Smiðjustígur (tel: 438 1450, <www.saeferdir.is>) runs ferries to Flatey and Hrappsey, as well as operating fjord trips and other excursions. Sæfari (tel: 461 3600), runs ferries from Dalvík to Grímsey in the summer.

Train Travel. There are no trains on Iceland.

R

RELIGION

Iceland has been Christian for more than 1,000 years. Ninety percent of the population adhere to the National Church of Iceland, which is evangelical Lutheran, and there are churches and chapels all over the country, even on some farms. About 1 percent of the population is Roman Catholic.

Reykjavík has two cathedrals and the imposing Hallgrímskirkja. Dómkirkjan, the Protestant cathedral (Austurvöllur, tel: 551 2113), holds communion services on Sunday at 11am. Kathólska Kirkjan, the Catholic cathedral (Túngata, tel: 552 5388), celebrates Mass in English on Sunday at 6pm. At Hallgrímskirkja (Skólavörduholt, tel: 510 1000), Sunday Mass is held at 11am.

T

TELEPHONES

The code for Iceland is +354, followed by a seven-digit number. There are no area codes. To call abroad from Iceland, dial 00, plus the country code. If you use the Iceland telephone book, remember that it lists people by their first names.

Payphones are found in post offices, filling (petrol) stations and on the street. These take coins or phone cards, which can be bought at post offices in various denominations.

There are three mobile-phone operators providing GSM and NMT services, with the latter covering more of the country than the former. Pre-paid cards can be bought at filling stations.

Useful numbers are as follows:
114: international directories
115: international operator
118: directories assistance

TIME DIFFERENCES

Iceland is on GMT all year round. Time in summer is as below.

Los Angeles	Chicago	New York	**Iceland**	London	Sydney
5am	7am	8am	**noon**	1pm	10pm

TIPPING

Service is always included in the bill, so tipping is not normally required. It is not usual to tip taxi drivers.

TOILETS

Iceland has an excellent plumbing system, and toilets are almost always clean and well maintained. There are toilets in restaurants, cafés and bars for customers, but public toilets are few and far between – there is only one in Reykjavík, close to the tourist office at the junction of Bankastræti and Lækjargata.

TOURIST INFORMATION

The tourist information structure is a little complex. The Icelandic Tourist Board (Lækjargata 3, Reykjavík, tel: 535 5500, <www.icetourist.is>), promotes Iceland abroad. The regional Tourist Information Centres are separately run, and some parts of the country also have Marketing Agencies. All the various offices offer more information than you could possibly need. Staff speak excellent English and are usually very helpful. Opening times vary, but in summer they open early and close around 7pm.

The Tourist Information Centre in Reykjavík is at Bankastræti 2, tel: 562 3045, <www.tourist.reykjavik.is> (open daily June–Aug 8.30am–6pm, Sept–May Mon–Fri 9am–5pm, Sat, Sun 10am–2pm).

In Akureyri, the Tourist Information Centre is at Strandgata 29, tel. 461 2915.

In the US, contact the Icelandic Tourist Office, 655 Third Avenue, New York, NY 10017, tel: 212 885 9700, <www.goiceland.org>.

There are no Icelandic Tourist Offices in Australia, Canada, Ireland, New Zealand, South Africa or the UK. Information can be obtained worldwide from the excellent <www.icetourist.is>.

W

WEBSITES AND INTERNET CAFÉS

Websites. Every business and organisation, large and small, now seems to have a website. In addition to those listed in the sections above, the following provide useful information before you arrive:

<www.east.is>

<www.northern.is>

<www.south.is>

<www.west.is>

<www.westfjords.is>

<www.tourist.reykjavik.is>

<www.eyeoniceland.com> (information, photographs, books and listings with useful links to specialist sites)

<www.icewhale.is> (Húsavík Whale Centre)

<www.natturuvernd.is> (Nature Conservation Agency site with valuable information on safety and protecting the environment)

<www.this.is/iceland> (tours, excursions, weather etc)

<www.whatson.is> (details of events)

<www.bluelagoon.is> (information on the Blue Lagoon)

<www.norvol.hi.is> (volcanoes in Iceland)

Internet Cafés. The cheapest way to get on to the Internet is at public libraries where access is free, although you may have to wait to get to a terminal. Internet cafés are springing up around the country, and costs vary – in some you pay for access, but the coffee is free.

Y

YOUTH HOSTELS

The Icelandic Youth Hostel Association (Sundlaugavegur 34, PO Box 1045, 121 Reykjavík, tel: 553 8110, fax: 588 9201, <www.hostel.is>) has 24 excellent hostels from which to choose. These are very popular and fill up quickly, so always book ahead. The association can provide a booklet listing hostels and the facilities they offer – most hostels have two- to six-bed rooms and family rooms. You can use your own sleeping-bag/linen or hire what you need. Good deals on car hire and excursions are also offered by the association.

Recommended Hotels

The range of hotel and hostel accommodation in Iceland is very wide indeed. In Reykjavík there are some very stylish, world-class hotels – with prices to match. Elsewhere in the country, with one or two exceptions, there are few hotels of real character, but what is lacking in terms of ambience is usually more than compensated by a stunning location. At the top end of the market, most hotels are fairly standard airport-style establishments. There is a reasonable selection of smaller, family-run hotels and guesthouses throughout the country, as well as budget accommodation for backpackers and hikers. Some schools double up as tourist accommodation during the holidays and this can be a very economical option.

High season is usually from the beginning of May until the beginning of September, when prices often double, and rooms can be hard to come by. Book well ahead if you want to be sure of the hotel of your choice. From the end of September some places close altogether, although you should be able to find a room in most towns. The bigger hotels are increasingly offering special activities, such as snow-mobiling, to attract visitors out of season.

The following guides provide an overview of where to stay: *Accommodation in Iceland*, from Áning Publications, Breiðvangi 3, 220 Hafnarfjörður, tel: 555 2405, and *Hotels and Guesthouses in Iceland*, from the Association of the Travel Industry, Hafnarstræti 20, 101 Reykjavík, tel: 511 8000, <www.saf.is>.

The price guidelines below are for a double room with bathroom in high season, including breakfast and tax, unless otherwise stated. Most hotels accept major credit cards. For making reservations, Iceland's country code is 354 (there are no local codes in Iceland).

$$$$	over 17,500 Ikr
$$$	15,000 Ikr–18,000 Ikr
$$	10,000–15,000 Ikr
$	below 10,000 Ikr

REYKJAVÍK

Álfhóll Guesthouse $ *Ránargata 8, tel: 898 1838, fax: 552 3838, <www.islandia.is/alf>*. A cosy little guesthouse a short distance from the centre, with clean, comfortable rooms and shared bathrooms. The name means 'Elves House', and the owners are always more than happy to tell you all you need to know about Iceland's trolls.

Hótel Borg $$$$ *Pósthússtræti 11, tel: 551 1440, fax: 551 1420, <www.hotelborg.is>*. This imposing building close to the Parliament was recently renovated to try to recreate the feel of the 1930s, when the hotel first opened, but many original art deco features have unfortunately been lost. The hotel was the site of the Icelandic rock music revival in the 1980s, although it's now a much grander affair.

Hótel Cabin $$ *Borgartún 32, tel: 511 6030, fax: 511 603*. Hótel Cabin is located a little out of the centre but has terrific views over the bay. Unusually, the owners promote rooms that face into the corridor, aiming at those who find the all-night summer sunshine keeps them awake. Brightly furnished, well-equipped rooms.

Hótel Holt $$$$ *Bergstaðastræti 37, tel: 552 5700, fax: 562 3025, <www.holt.is>*. Part of the Relais and Châteaux chain, this hotel is very elegant and comfortable, with great character and style. The public areas are an art-lover's delight, with the largest private collection of Icelandic paintings in existence. The rooms are well equipped, if a little small, and the restaurant is superb. A very special place, but at a price – and breakfast is extra.

Hótel Klöpp $$ *Klapparstigur 26, tel: 511 6062, fax: 511 6071, <www.centrehotels.is>*. Located right in the centre of town, this hotel has a cool, minimalist style, with lots of slate, wooden décor, large windows and brightly decorated bedrooms. The breakfast room is open all day for light snacks, but there is no restaurant.

Kríunes Guesthouse $ *Lake Elliðaárvatn, tel: 567 2245, fax: 567 2226*. The delightful setting beside the lake makes the short taxi drive out of the city to this tastefully converted former farmhouse worthwhile. Unusual hispanic décor. Kitchen facilities are available to guests.

Hótel Leifur Eríksson $$ *Skólavörðustígur 45, tel: 562 0800, fax: 562 0804, <hotel-leifur@vortex.is>.* Set right beneath the Hallgrímskirkja church, this is a friendly family-run place. It has basic but comfortable rooms and a snack bar serving light meals and drinks 24 hours a day.

Loftleiðir $$$ *City Airport, tel: 505 0900, fax: 505 0905, <www.icehotel.is/loftleidir>.* This Icelandair-owned hotel is conveniently situated for late arrivals or early departures from either of Reykjavík's two airports (buses run to the International Airport from here). It's quite a hike from the city centre, but it does have its own pool and sauna.

Luna Guesthouse $$ *Spítalastígur 1, tel: 511 2800, fax: 511 2801, <www.islandia.is/~luna>.* This place is a cut above the average guesthouse. It's an old family home, converted to provide elegant two-room apartments, each with a bathroom and a sofa-bed in the living room.

Óðinsvé $$$$ *Óðinstorg, tel: 511 6200, fax: 511 6201, <www.hotelodinsve.is>.* The pleasant, relaxed atmosphere and stylish but subtle decoration make this hotel, in a quiet residential quarter close to the centre, a comfortable place to stay. There are Internet connections, a trouser press and hair dryer in every room. The restaurant is run by a well-known Icelandic celebrity chef.

Room with a View $ *Laugavegur 18, tel/fax: 552 7262, <www.roomwithaview.is>.* For a good, cost-effective alternative to a hotel, try these pleasant apartments on the main shopping street. A kitchen and steambath are available to guests, and the balconies offer impressive views. Gay friendly.

Saga $$$ *Hagatorg, tel: 525 9900, fax: 525 9909, <www.radisson.com.* A Radisson-SAS hotel, with the usual business and leisure facilities and functional rooms of establishments in that group, and

popular for conferences. There are great views over the city from the skyline restaurant plus a geothermally heated pool on the roof.

Hotel Skjaldbreið $$ *Laugavegur 16, tel: 511 6060, fax: 511 6070, <www.centrehotels.is>.* On the main shopping street, this is the partner to the Hótel Klöpp, which is just round the corner. It's the less welcoming of the two, although the rooms are similar and the style is equally trendy.

SOUTH AND SOUTHEAST

Gistihúsið Árnanes $ *Airport road, Höfn, tel: 478 1550, fax: 478 1819, <www.arnanes.is>.* Here you'll find farm-stay accommodation in five separate wooden cabins, all run by a local artist, whose paintings and decorated wooden candlesticks are on display in the dining room. The rooms are spacious and comfortable, with a lovely rural feel.

Hótel Eldhestar $$ *Vellir, 810 Hveragerdi, tel: 480 4800, fax: 480 4801, <www.hoteleldhestar.is>.* This is Iceland's premier 'eco-hotel', a lovely single-storey wooden building surrounded by bushes and shrubs. The staff can offer plenty of advice on how to make the most of the environment and preserve it for the future; they can also arrange riding and golfing packages. The rooms are comfortable and all have computer connections and access to the garden; there are log fires in the communal areas. This is a non-smoking hotel with full disabled access.

Hótel Geysir $ *Haukadal Biskupstungum, 801 Selfoss, tel: 486 8915, fax: 486 8715, <www.geysircentre.is>.* Located right next to the world-famous geysers, this, the area's former sports academy, has been converted into a modern and very pleasant place to stay. It's a friendly, family-run establishment and gets very busy with tour groups in high season. There are hot tubs (accessible in summer only) and an outdoor pool.

Hreiðrið Guesthouse $ *Faxastígur, Heimaey, Westman Islands, tel: 481 1045, fax: 481 1414, <http:/tourist.eyjar.is>.* A popular alternative to the only hotel on Heimaey and very good value. Staying here feels like being taken into an Icelander's home.

Fosshótel Ingólfur $ *Ingólfshvoll, 810 Selfoss, tel: 483 5222, fax: 562 4001, <www.fosshotel.is>*. This is a great destination for horse-lovers, as there is a farm with 60 horses on the premises. All rooms have a private patio and hot tub – especially welcome after a day on horseback or hiking.

Hótel Kirkjubæjarklaustur $$$ *Klausturvegur 6, Kirkjubæjark-laustur, tel: 487 4900, fax: 487 4614, <www.icehotel.is/klaustur>*. Icelandair has built this large modern hotel in a town with literally one street, but it's very welcome as there is nothing else to this standard for some distance around. Out of season you could find you have the whole place to yourself. The friendly and helpful staff are always welcoming.

Hótel Lundi $ *Víkurbraut 26, Vík, tel: 487 1212, fax: 487 1404, <www.hotelpuffin.is>*. A delightful little place with a cosy dining room and bar. *Lundi* means puffin in Icelandic, and the owners, who are great nature enthusiasts, will be more than happy to tell you where to go and see the real things.

Hótel Þórshamar $$ *Vestmannabraut 28, Heimaey, Westman Islands, tel: 481 2900, fax: 481 1696, <www.hotel.eyjar.is>*. This is the only hotel in Heimaey (guesthouses are the norm on the island). There are videos and radios in the rooms in the main building – useful when the weather closes in – although not in their second, more basic, building down by the harbour.

Fosshótel Vatnajökull $$$ *Lindarbakki, 781 Höfn, tel: 478 2555, fax: 562 4001, <www.fosshotel.is>*. Situated outside the town, this hotel is well located for jeep tours on to the glacier.

EAST AND NORTHEAST

Hótel Björk $$$ *Hafnarstræti 67, Akureyri, tel: 461 3030, <www.hotelkea.is/english/bjork>*. Nothing to do with Iceland's most-famous singing export, this is a well-situated hotel in a quiet spot just outside the town centre overlooking the longest fjord in the country. The rooms are small, but pleasant enough.

Gistihúsið Egilsstöðum $$ *Lakeside, Egilsstaðir, tel: 471 1114, fax: 471 1266, <www.isholf.is/egilsstadir/hotel>*. This converted stone farmhouse aims to recreate the atmosphere of early 20th-century rural Iceland. The building itself dates from 1903, and its old-style parlour and collection of period artefacts all add to the effect. It's just west of the town on the shores of Lake Lögurinn. There are horses in the paddock.

Hótel Hérað $$$ *Sundurlinðungjalda, Egilsstaðir, tel: 471 1500, fax: 471 1501, <www.icehotel.is/herad>*. Part of the Icelandair chain, this is the only smart hotel in this area of the country. It's large and functional, and while it is somewhat lacking in character, it's still a welcome sight after a long day hiking.

Fosshótel Húsavík $$$ *Ketilsbraut 22, Húsavík, tel: 464 1220, fax: 464 2161, <www.fosshotel.is>*. The only decent-sized hotel in the whale-watching capital of Iceland. The staff can organise trips for you, and there is a welcoming bar to help you warm up on your return, as well as a good restaurant.

Hótel Kea $$$ *Hafnarstræti 87–9, Akureyri, tel: 460 2000, fax: 460 2060, <www.hotelkea.is>*. The largest and most comfortable hotel in Akureyri, close to all the town's restaurants and shops. The rooms are equipped with mini-bars and satellite television, and there is free internet access in the lobby.

Hótel Mývatn $$$ *Skútustaðir, 660 Mývatn, tel: 464 4164, fax: 464 4364,<www.myvatn.is>*. A modern, if rather austere, three-storey building with magnificent views over the lake. There are computer connections in every room, and the friendly staff will help to organise tours throughout the year.

Hótel Reynihlíð $$$ *Beside the old church, tel: 464 4170, fax: 464 4371, <www.reynihlid.is>*. This traditional family-run hotel has been extended many times to accommodate the growing number of tourists to the Lake Mývatn area. The newer rooms are smart and modern, and there is a lovely little café and bar in the adjoining Old Farm building that can get very lively in the evenings. It's important to book well ahead in high season. The hotel also offers sleeping-bag accommodation.

Fosshótel Reyðarfjörður $$$ *Búðareyri 6, Reyðarfjöður, tel: 474 1600, fax: 562 4001, <www.fosshotel.is>.* This bright new hotel, opened in 1999, is geared up for conference business but still caters for skiers in the winter, and hunters and fishermen in the late summer and autumn.

WEST AND NORTHWEST

Fosshótel Bifröst $$ *311 Borgarfjörður, tel: 433 3090, fax: 562 4001, <www.fosshotel.is>.* Housed in the local business school in Bifröst, this hotel is only open in the summer when the students are away. The children's playground and hot tubs are added bonuses.

Hótel Tindastóll $$$ *Lindargata 3, Sauðárkrókur, tel: 453 5002, fax: 453 5388, <www.hoteltindastoll.com>.* Built in 1884, this is not only the oldest hotel in Iceland but also one of the nicest and most unusual. With its stone walls and timber beams it retains a great sense of history. The original front door is still intact, and there are all kinds of antique artefacts dotted throughout. Every room has a different shape, colour and name, but they are all a good size and have modern amenities including computer points, DVDs and power showers. Marlene Dietrich stayed here while entertaining the troops during World War II.

Vogur Guesthouse $ *Flatey Island, tel: 438 1413.* This guesthouse is a lovely old place, dating from 1885, with winding wooden staircases and low ceilings. It was once a home for visiting clergymen, but is now open to all. It gets booked up in summer, so call ahead and reserve. There are great views out over the harbour from the upper rooms.

Recommended Restaurants

There is no uniform Icelandic dining experience – instead, the standard, price and even availability of restaurants varies dramatically from place to place and season to season. Reykjavík has some truly world-class chefs, serving superb meals in very fine establishments. At the same time, fashionable eateries, where the stylish décor is as important as what's on your plate, have been springing up all over the capital, as well as in places such as Akureyri. Outside these two cities, you are more likely to have to choose between hotel restaurants, some of which can be very good, or smaller, less-ambitious places, where the food tends to be wholesome rather than exciting. In some relatively large towns there may be little more than a pizzeria and a grill bar attached to a service station, especially out of season.

Wherever you are in Iceland, you won't be far from a harbour, and the catch of the day is often the tastiest and best-value option on the menu. Helpings are usually large, so don't over-order. Wine is ruinously expensive almost everywhere, and a bottle can sometimes cost more than the meal itself. Beer isn't cheap, but it's a lot better value than wine.

Many restaurants offer good-value special tourist menus or lunch or dinner buffets. There is usually an unlimited supply of fresh bread and butter, as well as a jug of cold tap water. Prices are lower for lunch. Children under six years old usually eat for free and six- to 12-year-olds are charged half price.

The prices indicated below are for a starter, main course and dessert, but not wine, per person. Tax at 24.5 percent and service are always included in the bill, although if you wish you can leave a little more for exceptional service. Almost all restaurants will accept most major credit cards.

$$$$	over 10,000 Ikr
$$$	5,000–10,000 Ikr
$$	2,500–5,000 Ikr
$	below 2,500 Ikr

REYKJAVÍK

Apótek $$$ *Austurstræti 16, tel: 575 7900.* This is the kind of place where you will spot Reykjavík's young, fashionable folk, who don't mind paying a bit over the odds. It's very trendy, with low lighting and soft music, and gets pretty lively at weekends. Located on the site of a former chemist – hence the name – Apótek is still a little clinical for some tastes. However, the food, especially the fish-based starters, is consistently good, and the menus are changed every four months to keep people coming back for more.

Hótel Borg $$$$ *Pósthússtræti 11, tel: 551 1440.* Eat here in art deco splendour and imagine that you are back in the 1930s – except, of course, for the distinctly 21st-century prices. The menu is eclectic and includes delights such as slow-cooked pigeon with exotic fruits, and duck liver paté.

Caruso $ *Pingholtsstræti 1, tel: 562 7335.* Cosy Italian bistro on three floors in the centre of town, doing good pizzas and pasta dishes and healthy salads. Very welcoming with no pretensions.

Grænn Kostur $ *Skólavörðustígur 8, tel: 552 2028.* A terrific little vegetarian restaurant with great-value, wholesome food. There is a choice between two main courses of the day, although you can have a little of each, and the menu changes daily. The famed garlic and chilli sauce is always available, however, and people come for miles to taste it. Delicious banana, apple and carrot cakes to finish off the meal.

Hótel Holt $$$$ *Bergstaðastræti 37, tel: 552 5700.* Arguably the best restaurant in the capital with a magnificent, if rather dark, dining room full of Icelandic art. The chef uses fresh local produce, including a wide range of fish, reindeer and lamb, and presents the dishes with creativity. The bill will be as eye-watering as the food is mouth-watering, but you won't be disappointed.

Jómfrúin $ *Lækjargata 4, tel: 551 0100.* Excellent-value Danish open sandwiches on rye or French bread with 150 different toppings that range from crispy bacon and liver paté to caviar and eggs. A healthy and inexpensive lunch option near the tourist office.

Lækjarbrekka $$$ *Bankastræti 2, tel: 551 4430.* This is Icelandic cuisine at its very best in one of the oldest buildings (dating from 1835) in Reykjavík. There's a romantic dining room downstairs and a more modern one above. The vast menu has more than 40 dishes, mostly featuring Icelandic seafood and lamb. The lobster is superb, and the home-baked puddings are worth leaving space for.

Þrir Frakkar $$ *Baldursgata 14, tel: 552 3939.* If you don't mind the plastic fish on the walls and the slightly chaotic feel of this little back-street French bistro, you will enjoy good food with generous helpings in a friendly atmosphere. Try the smoked puffin as a starter; the monkfish with vegetables and pesto is also delicious.

Prima Vera $$$ *Austurstræti 9, tel: 561 8555.* Come here for top-class Italian cooking with sun-dried tomatoes, puréed mushrooms and balsamic vinegar featuring strongly on the menu. There's a large, min-imalist dining room on the first floor, where even the slightly brusque service is reminiscent of Italy. The menu isn't extensive, but the quality is uniformly good, and the chocolate puddings are to die for.

Síggí Hall $$$ *Óðinstorg, tel: 511 6200.* Run by and named after Iceland's most well-known celebrity chef, this place has won inter-national praise for its originality. The portions and presentation are of the *nouvelle-cuisine* variety, but the food is all organic. The wooden floors and crisp white tablecloths give the restaurant a classy feel that's in keeping with the standard of the food.

Skólabrú $$$$ *Skólabrú 1, tel: 562 4455.* Dining in this family house from the early 20th century makes you feel as if you could be eating in somebody's home. Real old-style service and beauti-fully presented food. The menu mixes Icelandic and international dishes, with an emphasis on seafood, duck and game.

Vegamót $$ *Vegamótastígur 4, tel: 511 3040.* Noisy, fashionable hang-out for Reykjavík's young crowd, where the staff can even text you their special offers. The menu is of the chicken, burgers and *burritos* variety, but the helpings are generous, and the atmosphere swings between hot and just plain warm. It's great for brunch, especially after a hard night's clubbing.

SOUTH AND SOUTHEAST

Blue Lagoon Restaurant $$ *Blue Lagoon, Grindavík, tel: 420 8800.* Eat overlooking the thermal spa at this now world-famous spot. The menu uses fish brought ashore at the nearby harbour, but presents it in a variety of international dishes including *bouillabaisse* and curried cod. There are also chicken and pasta dishes, hamburgers and a children's menu. Best enjoyed after, rather than before, a dip in the hot waters.

Hótel Geysir $$ *Haukadal Biskupstungum, 801 Selfoss, tel: 486 8915.* This hotel's large dining room gets very busy in summer with tour groups. It offers an excellent, if unusual menu, including breast of guillemot and peking duck. The locally caught salmon is superb, as is the bread baked underground in the traditional Icelandic fashion. Good two- and three-course specials. Try to leave room for the sumptuous desserts.

EAST AND NORTHEAST

Apótek $$$ *Strandgata 11, Akureyri, tel: 462 1860.* An off-shoot of the trendy Reykjavík restaurant *(see page 138)*, showing Akureyri's efforts to keep up with the capital in terms of fashion. The décor is stark and almost all in white, but the atmosphere warms up once the restaurant gets busy. The food is good – dishes include local ingredients served with an international twist.

Fridrik V $$$ *Strandgata 7, Akureyri, tel: 461 5775.* A recent addition to the town's increasingly fashionable eateries. There is a friendly café on the ground floor, with a more formal restaurant upstairs, where the service is a little haughty at times, but the food is excellent. Don't eat all day if you want to try the four-course gourmet platter. The smoked pork with sun-glazed silver onions and blue-cheese sauce makes a nice change to the usual Icelandic fare of lamb and reindeer. Closed at lunchtime.

Gamli Bærinn $ *Beside Hotel Reynihlíð, Mývatn, tel: 464 4170.* The name means 'old farm', and the building, which dates from 1912, is by the architect who designed Reykjavík's Parliament. The place is now a delightful little restaurant and café, where fantastic char soup (char being a type of red trout) is served. There are always specials on the blackboard, and they have live jazz and local bands at the weekend.

Café Menning $–$$ *Hafnarbraut 14, Dalvík, tel: 466 1213.* A quirky little café and restaurant with regular live music.

WEST AND NORTHWEST

Café Riis $$ *Hafnarbraut 39, Holmavík, tel: 451 3567, fax: 451 3557.* Renovated old wooden house in the town centre, where fish, lamb, burgers and sandwiches are on the menu. Check the opening hours before setting out.

Hótel Buðir Restaurant $$$ *Main road, Buðir, tel: 435 6700.* Reopened in 2002 after major renovations, this place is regaining its former reputation for top-class cuisine. Seafood and game predominate, including coconut-roasted clams and guillemot with blueberry sauce.

Hótel Flókalundur $$–$$$ *Vatnsfjörður, tel: 456 2011.* This is the only restaurant in the vicinity but it often serves excellent food. Closed in winter.

Hótel Ísafjörður Restaurant $$$ *Silfurtorg 2, tel: 456 4111.* In the spacious, bright dining room at this hotel, you can enjoy fish straight from the quay just a couple of blocks away, plus superb views overlooking the fjord and the mountains behind. However, don't expect to be eating with many of the locals, as the prices make this a place for the hotel's own guests and other relatively affluent tourists. The standard of the food is consistently good.